TRANSDISCIPLINARY TEAMING
in Early Intervention/
Early Childhood Special Education

navigating together with families and children

Jennifer L. Kilgo, Editor

association for childhood education international

17904 GEORGIA AVE., STE. 215, OLNEY, MARYLAND, 20832

800-423-3563 • WWW.ACEI.ORG

Bruce Herzig, ACEI Editor
Anne Bauer, ACEI Editor
Deborah Jordan Kravitz, Design and Production

Copyright (c) 2006, Association for Childhood Education International
17904 Georgia Ave., Ste. 215, Olney MD 20832

Library of Congress Cataloging-in-Publication Data
Transdisciplinary teaming in early intervention/early childhood special education :
navigating together with families and children / Jennifer L. Kilgo, editor.
    p. cm.
 Includes bibliographical references.
 ISBN 0-87173-168-1
 1. Children with disabilities--Education (Early childhood) 2. Early childhood special
education. 3. Special education--Parent participation. 4. Health care teams. I. Kilgo,
Jennifer Lynn.

 LC4019.3.T73 2005
 371.9'0472--dc22

2005035233

Dedication

This book is dedicated to J. David Sexton, who inspired, mentored, and collaborated with the editor and authors of this book. His vision began our work with transdisciplinary teaming at the University of Alabama at Birmingham. His initial work laid the ground for two Department of Education/Division of Personnel Preparation grants that are still funding our efforts to make a difference in the lives of children with disabilities and their families. In 1995, David and Jennifer simultaneously began their teaching and research at UAB and immediately began their work with the authors of this book to establish transdisciplinary personnel preparation in early intervention/early childhood special education. This book would not have been possible without David. We are truly grateful and dedicate this work to his memory.

Table of Contents

Preface

Jennifer L. Kilgo

Teamwork is a central component of the larger system of services and supports for young children with disabilities and their families. Professionals and family members make up teams that, when effective, not only recognize their discipline-specific roles in the early intervention/education system but also develop close working relationships that evolve over time. Transdisciplinary teamwork, as described in this book, involves team members who perform tasks collaboratively by sharing information and roles. Mutually agreed-upon goals/outcomes are developed and information, knowledge, and skills are transferred across disciplinary boundaries. Although transdisciplinary teamwork can be challenging, it remains essential to ensuring that children and their families receive the best services possible.

The University of Alabama at Birmingham (UAB) is fortunate to have a cadre of highly competent and committed faculty members who have worked together in the development of this book. The contributors collectively represent many years of experience in teamwork as part of the graduate training programs at UAB emphasizing services for young children with disabilities. The focus of the program is on team-based learning for students, representing multiple disciplines, who will become members of transdisciplinary teams. As a result of our collaborative experiences over the last 10 years, this book was developed to share our beliefs about the importance of teamwork. We have taught our students how to function as team members and, as faculty members representing various disciplines, we have functioned as transdisciplinary team members ourselves.

This book is designed to provide an introduction to transdisciplinary teaming. The book begins with a description of, and rationale for, a transdisciplinary service delivery model in early intervention/education. What follows is a discussion of how to establish successful teams, given the myriad challenges often faced by teams as they provide services for young children with disabilities and their families. A case study of the Gonzales family is included to illustrate the individual differences, strengths, concerns, priorities, and resources of families. Issues faced by the Gonzales family are woven throughout the remaining chapters to demonstrate how a team-based approach can be used to meet the unique needs of families.

Chapters 4-10 were developed to provide a description of the various professional disciplines that may provide early intervention/education services including, but not limited to, early childhood special education, general early childhood education, speech-language pathology, audiology, occupational therapy, physical therapy, nursing, and English language learning. Information is provided about what others should know about each of these disciplines, contributions to the team, issues and challenges faced by the discipline, as well as specific information related to the case study of the Gonzales family. Chapter 11 centers on how professionals from various disciplines and families can work together to create a well-functioning team, with the focus on the young child within the context of the family. The final chapter is devoted to personnel preparation and describes how early childhood teachers (general and special) and related service personnel (e.g., physical therapists, nurses, speech-language pathologists, occupational therapists) can learn and develop together in order to become well-functioning team members.

As noted earlier, it is our belief that transdisciplinary teaming is a vital component of early intervention/education. Our hope is that this text illustrates the importance of transdisciplinary teamwork, the many benefits of a team-based approach, and strategies for making high-quality team-based services a reality for young children with disabilities and their families.

Chapter 1

Overview of Transdisciplinary Teaming in Early Intervention/ Early Childhood Special Education

 *Jennifer L. Kilgo*

Early intervention/early childhood special education is a rapidly growing and ever-changing field. Each year, a growing number of children with known or suspected disabilities are served in programs throughout the United States and in other countries. Early intervention/early childhood special education (EI/ECSE) spans the period from birth through age 8 and, therefore, includes early intervention, preschool special education, and early primary special education. The children receiving EI/ECSE services are diverse in terms of their ages; their socioeconomic, cultural, linguistic, ethnic, and religious backgrounds; and their delays and/or disabilities. Children with special needs may have a wide range of disabilities, including physical, behavioral, cognitive, language, social-emotional, or health-related disabilities. In the United States, these children usually qualify for early intervention, early childhood special education, and related services provided under the special education law known as the Individuals With Disabilities Education Improvement Act (IDEA) (2004), although the laws and services vary in other countries.

The expertise of professionals with a range of backgrounds is required in order to meet the diverse specific, and often complex, needs of young children with known or suspected disabilities. Obviously, one or two professionals will be unable to provide everything that a child and family may need. The skills of professionals from the disciplines of early childhood education (general and special), physical therapy, occupational therapy, speech-language pathology, and nursing are often needed. In addition, the skills of professionals from other disciplines, such as English language learning, nutrition, vision, audiology, school psychology, and social work, may be required, depending on the child's and family's needs. Even less traditional disciplines may be needed in unique situations (e.g., respiratory therapy). Regardless of which and how many disciplines are required, these professionals must function interdependently in order to be as effective as possible. The notion is that different perspectives lead to better decisions and services. The purpose of this book is to describe how professionals from multiple disciplines can function as a team to meet the needs of young children with disabilities and their families.

This chapter underscores recommended practices emphasizing the need for team-based services in early intervention/early childhood special education. The discussion focuses on the various team-based models that have been used in the field over the years. Specific details are provided regarding a transdisciplinary service delivery model, which is most often the preferred model for EI/ECSE settings (McWilliam, 2005).

Recommended Practices

As the number and diversity of children and families served by EI/ECSE programs have grown, recommended practices have evolved to meet the changing needs of

overview

the field. Appropriate practices have become more clearly defined regarding how services should be delivered, what represents recommended practice (Sandall, Hemmeter, Smith, & McLean, 2005), and how personnel should be prepared to provide effective services in the 21st century (Kilgo & Bruder, 1997; Stayton, Miller, & Dinnebeil, 2002).

Recommended practices in EI/ECSE emphasize that every effort should be made for young children with known or suspected disabilities to be included in natural learning environments. According to IDEA, *natural environments* are those settings that are natural or typical for the child's age peers who have no disabilities. Such settings include homes, playgrounds, child care, grocery stores, and play groups. This often translates to home, community settings, child care centers, preschools, Head Start programs, and early primary settings such as kindergarten classrooms. Some locations that are *not* considered to be natural environments include health care settings, segregated settings, and clinics. Although much discussion over the years addressed the benefits and challenges of inclusive early childhood programs (Bredekamp, 1993; Buysse & Bailey, 1993; Childress, 2004; Fox & Hanline, 1993; McLean & Odom, 1993; Miller, 1992; Peterson & Beloin, 1998), an inclusive setting is no longer a rarity as a service delivery option. Legislation, such as IDEA in the United States, has provided continued support of inclusive programs for young children with developmental delays or disabilities. With services being provided in inclusive environments, this calls for general early childhood educators to be members of the team providing EI/ECSE.

Recommended practice suggests that a team-based orientation permeate all aspects of service delivery to include assessment, team meetings and program planning, related services, intervention activities, and service coordination (Miller & Stayton, 2005). This approach is a sharp contrast to services of the past, when coordination, collaboration, and teamwork were rarely demonstrated. To illustrate the mistakes of the past, a great cartoon was developed by Michael Giangreco and illustrated by Kevin Ruelle, titled "Severely Dysfunctional Team." One team member is walking away with the child's legs, another with his head, and another with his arms. With a team like this, each team member addresses a different area of need and

SEVERELY DYSFUNCTIONAL TEAM

From: Giangreco, M. F. (1998). *Ants in his pants: Absurdities and realities of special education.* Minnetonka, MN: Peytral Publications. www.peytral.com Reprinted with permission:

Figure 1.1

Comparison of Three Team Models

	Multidisciplinary	Interdisciplinary	Transdisciplinary
Assessment	Separate assessments by team members	Separate assessments by team members	Team members and family conduct a comprehensive developmental assessment together
Parent Participation	Parents meet with individual team members	Parents meet with team or team representative	Parents are full, active, and participating members of the team
Service/Intervention Plan (e.g., IFSP, IEP) Development	Team members develop separate plans for their discipline	Team members share their separate plans with one another	Team members and the parents develop a service plan based on family priorities, needs, and resources
Service/Intervention Plan (e.g., IFSP, IEP) Responsibility	Team members are responsible for implementing their section of the plan	Team members are responsible for sharing information with one another, as well as for implementing their section of the plan	Team members are responsible and accountable for how the primary service provider implements the plan
Service/Intervention Plan (e.g., IFSP, IEP) Implementation	Team members implement the part of the service plan related to their discipline	Team members implement their section of the plan and incorporate other sections, where possible	A primary service provider is assigned to implement the plan with the family
Lines of Communication	Informal lines	Periodic case-specific team meetings	Regular team meeting where continuous transfer of information, knowledge, and skills are shared among team members
Guiding Philosophy	Team members recognize the importance of contributions from other disciplines	Team members are willing and able to develop, share, and be responsible for providing services that are a part of the total service plan	Team members make a commitment to teach, learn, and work together across discipline boundaries to implement unified service plan
Staff Development	Independent and within their discipline	Independent within as well as outside of their discipline	An integral component of team meetings for learning across disciplines and team building

From: Woodruff, G., & McGonigel, M. J. (1998). Early intervention team approaches: The transdisciplinary model. In J. B. Jordan, J. J. Gallagher, P. L. Hutinger, & M. B. Karnes (Eds.), *Early childhood special education: Birth to three* (p. 166). Reston, VA: Council for Exceptional Children. Reprinted with permission.

Table 1.1

there is no collaboration among the team members. On a dysfunctional team, the members individually develop their own goals/outcomes and objectives/strategies before the meeting and present them to the team. Fortunately, team-based practices have evolved and have definitely improved over the years. Traditional medical-model practices, in which different team members perform largely independently, are antithetical to recommended practices in EI/ECSE (McWilliam, 2005).

Team-based Models

Early intervention/early childhood special education involves collective responsibility, meaning that teamwork is needed to provide exemplary services to young children with special needs and their families (Allen, Holm, & Schieflebusch, 1978; Bruder, 1996; Campbell, 1987; McWilliam, 2005). As described earlier, the *team* consists of individuals from a variety of disciplines and backgrounds (e.g., early childhood special educator, general early childhood educator, physical therapist, occupational therapist, speech-language pathologist, nurse, physician, school psychologist, paraeducator), depending on the needs of the child, who are responsible for providing services to the child and family. In addition, the team includes the parents themselves (or guardians), who are central members of the transdisciplinary team.

Carpenter, King-Sears, and Keys (1998) describe structure and function as key elements of EI/ECSE teams. *Structure* refers to the specific members of the team—their organization and roles. *Function* includes the different activities in which members engage, such as assessment, intervention/service plan development, intervention/service plan implementation, communication, and so forth. The team structure used (multidisciplinary, interdisciplinary, or transdisciplinary) affects the functions incorporated into each team model, as well as the kinds of programs they provide for the children served (Carpenter et al., 1998; Galentine & Seery, 1999). The differences between these three team models are found in the hierarchy of membership and the manner in which they assess and plan children's outcomes. Multidisciplinary and interdisciplinary teams are known for having clear hierarchies of power and providing isolated assessment, planning, and intervention processes for each profession represented on the team. The transdisciplinary team model, the preferred model for early intervention/education settings, differs significantly from the other two models mentioned (multidisciplinary and interdisciplinary). Table 1.1 compares and contrasts multidisciplinary, interdisciplinary, and transdisciplinary team models. The transdisciplinary team model is described in greater detail in the section that follows.

Transdisciplinary Team Model

The transdisciplinary model assumes that all team members, including families, are part of the team structure. Professionals from different disciplines work together, with one person serving as the primary contact with the family. The primary contact uses strategies that the other team members provide, and the other team members have direct contact with the child and family only as necessary (e.g., for assessment, demonstration, progress reporting). Each member contributes equally to team functioning, is open to exchanging existing roles and acquiring new roles, and is committed to providing culturally competent, family-based services in natural environments for children with delays or disabilities. Collaboration, cooperation, and coordination among team members in the process of assessment, program development, and service delivery are hallmarks of team processes. The team members jointly identify the goals/outcomes, with discipline-specific goals/outcomes woven into the larger team goals.

The transdisciplinary approach currently is considered recommended practice because 1) it prevents the fragmentation of services along disciplinary lines, 2) it avoids duplication of services, 3) it views the whole child's development as integrated, and 4) it emphasizes the importance of the family as equal, contributing members of the team (Losardo & Notari-Sylverson, 2001; McWilliam, 2005).

Participation on transdisciplinary teams often requires personal and professional change on the part of team members in order for the team to function effectively. Transdisciplinary team members must accept families as equal team members, practice role release, and put discipline-specific goals secondary to team goals. It is important for transdisciplinary team members to be prepared in a manner that enables holistic vision and support for combined team efforts, rather than isolated, multiple, professional directives for families (Carpenter et al., 1998; Galentine & Seery, 1999; Hanft & Anzalone, 2001; Roberts-DeGennaro, 2002). When team members learn to practice within these parameters, there is less of the fragmentation and compartmentalization of services that is so often seen in other team models (Hinojosa et al., 2001; Ogletree, 2001; Roberts-DeGennaro, 2002).

A critical component of effective transdisciplinary teams is continuous communication among all team members. Ongoing communication is essential for maintaining a consistent approach to meeting the changing needs of the child, who is always considered within the context of the family. As one mother described, "The therapists and teachers must remember that the child is part of an entire family. If children are viewed in isolation and the team doesn't understand what the rest of the child's life is like and what's going on with the family, there's no way the process will work. And the only way they will know what's really going on is through communication with the parents."

On the transdisciplinary team, professionals from different disciplines, alongside the family, share roles and responsibilities and purposely cross discipline boundaries when they assess, plan, provide intervention, and monitor progress. All participants learn from one another and work together to accomplish the goals/outcomes of each child and family. This, of course, means that team members must be willing to share their knowledge with each other and be open to acquiring new skills (McWilliam, 2005). All team members must develop skills in problem solving, conflict resolution, and team consensus-building in order for the work of the team to be accomplished.

Benefits of a Transdisciplinary Model

The type of teamwork from educators, therapists, families, etc., described in this chapter makes inclusion possible. Integrated therapy represents recommended practice today and occurs when transdisciplinary teams deliver related services in inclusive settings. In other words, related services are provided to the child within the routines and activities of the natural setting (Davis, Kilgo, & Gamel-McCormick, 1998; Sandall, Hemmeter, Smith, & McLean, 2005). For example, during snack time in an inclusive preschool classroom, the speech-language pathologist may work with the child on his or her communication goals, such as verbalizing or signing a request for juice and other snack items, while also supporting social exchanges that occur during snack time. The physical therapist can provide input regarding the child's ambulation to the table where the snack will be served, and the occupational therapist may provide recommendations for proper positioning of adaptive eating utensils. In this way, the child is not pulled from the classroom for isolated therapy and can participate in the regular routines. The teacher can implement the therapists' suggestions during the everyday activities of the early childhood program, and the parents and other caregivers can do the same at home or in the community. Integrated therapeutic activities can provide the child with many opportunities to practice and generalize new skills in natural settings where they will be needed. It is easy to see why transdisciplinary teamwork and integrated therapy provided within the natural environment are central to successful inclusion.

Overview of Remainder of Text

This book is designed to provide an introduction to transdisciplinary teaming in early intervention/early childhood special education. First, the focus is on a description of, and rationale for, a transdisciplinary service delivery model, followed by a discussion of some of the issues and challenges faced by teams. A case study describes a child and family, and the services they receive, illustrating the need for a team-based approach. A description follows of some of the various disciplines involved in EI/ECSE and what others should know about each of these disciplines. The discussion then centers on how the various disciplines can work together to create a well-functioning team, with the focus on the young child within the context of the family. Transdisciplinary personnel preparation is described to illustrate how early childhood educators (general and special) and related service personnel (e.g., physical therapists, nurses, speech-language pathologists, occupational therapists) can be prepared to provide transdisciplinary services.

References

Allen, K. E., Holm, V. J., & Schieflebusch, R. L. (1978). *Early intervention: A team approach*. Baltimore: University Park Press.

Bredekamp, S. (1993). The relationship between early childhood education and early childhood special education: Healthy marriage or family feud? *Topics in Early Childhood Special Education, 13*(3), 258-273.

Bruder, M. R. (1996). Interdisciplinary collaboration in service delivery. In R. A. McWilliam (Ed.), *Rethinking pull-out services in early intervention: A professional resource* (pp. 27-48). Baltimore: Paul H. Brookes.

Buysse, V., & Bailey, D. B. (1993). Behavioral and developmental outcomes in young children with disabilities in integrated and segregated settings: A review of comparative studies. *The Journal of Special Education, 26*, 434-461.

Campbell, P. H. (1987). The integrated programming team: An approach for coordination professionals of various disciplines in programs for students with severe and multiple handicaps. *Journal of the Association for Persons With Severe Handicaps, 12*, 107-116.

Carpenter, S., King-Sears, M., & Keys, S. G. (1998). Counselors + educators + families as a transdisciplinary team = more effective inclusion for students with disabilities. *Professional School Counseling, 2*(1), 1-10.

Childress, D. C. (2004). Special instruction and natural environments: Best practices in early intervention. *Infants and Young Children, 17*, 162-170.

Davis, M., Kilgo, J., & Gamel-McCormick, M. (1998). *Young children with special needs: A developmentally appropriate approach*. Boston: Allyn & Bacon.

Fox, L., & Hanline, M. F. (1993). A preliminary evaluation of learning within developmentally appropriate early childhood settings. *Topics in Early Childhood Special Education, 13*(3), 308-327.

Galentine, J. K., & Seery, M. E. (1999). Achieving role expansion and release: Conversation strategies used by one transdisciplinary team. *Infant-Toddler Intervention: The Transdisciplinary Journal, 9*(1), 17-38.

Hanft, B., & Anzalone, M. (2001). Issues in professional development: Preparing and supporting occupational therapists in early childhood. *Infants and Young Children, 13*, 67-78.

Hinojosa, J., Bedell, G., Buchholz, E., Charles, J., Shigaki, I., & Bicchieri, S. (2001). Team collaboration: A case study of an early intervention team. *Qualitative Health Research, 11*, 206-220.

Individuals With Disabilities Education Improvement Act, 20 U.S.C. §602 (2004).

Kilgo, J., & Bruder, M. B. (1997). Creating new visions in institutions of higher education: Interdisciplinary approaches to personnel preparation in early intervention. In P. J. Winton, J. A. McCollum, & C. Catlett (Eds.), *Reforming personnel preparation in early intervention: Issues, models, and practical strategies* (pp. 81-101). Baltimore: Paul H. Brookes.

Losardo, A., & Notari-Sylverson, A. (2001). *Alternative approaches to assessing young children*. Baltimore: Paul H. Brookes.

McLean, M. E., & Odom, S. L. (1993). Practices for young children with and without disabilities: A comparison of DEC and NAEYC identified practices. *Topics in Early Childhood Special Education, 13*(3), 274-292.

McWilliam, R. A. (2005). Recommended practices in interdisciplinary models. In S. Sandall, M. L. Hemmeter, B. Smith, & M. McLean (Eds.), *DEC recommended practices for early intervention/early childhood special education* (pp. 47-54). Longmont, CO: Sopris West.

Miller, P. (1992). Segregated programs of teacher education in early childhood: Immoral and inefficient practice. *Topics in Early Childhood Special Education, 11*(4), 39-52.

Miller, P., & Stayton, V. (2005). Recommended practices in personnel preparation. In S. Sandall, M. L. Hemmeter, B. Smith, & M. McLean (Eds.), *DEC recommended practices for early intervention/early childhood special education* (pp. 77-88). Longmont, CO: Sopris West.

Ogletree, B. T. (2001). Team-based delivery for students with disabilities. *Intervention in School & Clinics, 36*(3), 138-146.

Peterson, M., & Beloin, K. S. (1998). Teaching the inclusive teacher: Restructuring the mainstreaming course in teacher education. *Teacher Education and Special Education, 21*(4), 306-318.

Roberts-DeGennaro, M. (2002). An interdisciplinary training model in the field of early intervention. *Social Work in Education, 18*(1), 20-30.

Sandall, S., Hemmeter, M., Smith, B., & McLean, M. (2005). *DEC recommended practices for early intervention/early childhood special education.* Longmont, CO: Sopris West.

Stayton, V., Miller, P., & Dinnebeil, L. (2002). *Personnel preparation in early childhood special education.* Longmont, CO: Sopris West.

Woodruff, G., & McGonigel, M. J. (1998). Early intervention team approaches: The transdisciplinary model. In J. B. Jordan, J. J. Gallagher, P. L. Hutinger, & M. B. Karnes (Eds.), *Early childhood special education: Birth to three* (p. 166). Reston, VA: Council for Exceptional Children.

Chapter 2

HOW TO ESTABLISH
SUCCESSFUL TEAMS

 — *Laura Vogtle*

M ost transdisciplinary teams face some challenges in supporting young children with known or suspected disabilities, and their families. This chapter describes how to establish a successful team and then discusses the many concerns and sources of conflict that transdisciplinary teams may face. Such issues as role release, service delivery, family-based services, and culturally appropriate practices are addressed, with attention to the sources of conflicts and steps that can be taken to prevent and deal with such conflicts.

Establishing Successful Teams

Bens (1999) states that the initial steps to establishing a successful team include taking time for member introductions, developing team rules of conduct, defining appropriate team behaviors, and outlining decision-making strategies. These steps enable team members to become familiar with each other and to develop the mutual support and honest communication that Ogletree (2001) indicates is important for team success. Transdisciplinary team members need to be able to trust each other enough to be vulnerable and honest in their interactions over time. Galentine and Seery (1999) use the metaphor of marriage, describing the team interactions as "a sort of working intimacy, a marriage which promotes open discourse and receptive participants" (p. 28). Rothermich, Kinnear, and Beck (1996) underscore the need for a sense of shared purpose developed through team tasks, such as establishing the mission statement and periodically revisiting and updating it. Hinojosa et al. (2001) studied a team that, due to administrative constraints, did not have the opportunity to develop the elements of a successful team discussed earlier, with resulting interactions that are illustrative of the difficulties that can occur. Lack of time to build common purpose and communication, pull-out service delivery practices by the therapists, lack of reciprocal respect for team members' roles, and struggles with inclusion of family members as part of the team were all challenges described as interfering with the outcomes of the intervention.

Ogletree (2001) identified six core attributes of good teams (see Table 2.1). A review of these attributes will demonstrate their interconnectedness. The mission statement stems from an agreement among team members as to the purpose of the team. Family-centeredness is a core value that is central to transdisciplinary teams and reflects the value that team members place on problem solving with families to provide optimum services for their children. Open and honest communication leads to the attributes of mutual support and familiarity expected between team members. Good team leadership and coordination provide the basis for honest and open communication, mutual support, and respect. As a team works together in a positive environment, the familiarity that ensues evolves and cements the relationships among members. All of these traits contribute to a nurturing environment in which personal growth on the part of team members is promoted, resulting in improved services for children with disabilities (Galentine & Seery, 1999).

Challenges to Transdisciplinary Teams

Virtually all professionals who provide services to children serve on many teams over the span of their careers. Most of us can remember teams on which we particularly enjoyed serving, as well as teams we would not chose to be part of, given the choice. The next section highlights particular aspects of transdisciplinary teams that can prove to be stumbling blocks for all of the team members, families and professionals alike.

Role Release. One particularly challenging aspect of transdisciplinary teams is role release. This practice requires members of various professions to be comfortable teaching their intervention practices to other professionals and reciprocally learning and delivering interventions from other fields. Galentine and Seery (1999) describe role release as a developmental process consisting of role extension, role enrichment, role expansion, role release, and role support—all steps leading to reciprocal role-sharing among team members (see Table 2.2).

The medical model training that nurses, physical therapists, and occupational therapists often undergo presents a hurdle to successful role release. This kind of preparation deals with the person being served as a passive recipient of care, which is directed by a physician. There is a clear hierarchy in the medical model, which dictates that the physician makes the final decisions; the individual client is the focus of treatment rather than a part of a family system in which all members are considered.

As more physical and occupational therapists are employed in school system settings, the medical training context has been de-emphasized to some extent. McEwen and Shelden (1995) suggest that current practice paradigms in physical therapy have eliminated the focus on medical model service delivery. However, their discussion continues to ignore issues of team building and collaboration, instead emphasizing discipline-specific characteristics. Professional practice in educational settings introduces therapists and nurses to both a different service delivery paradigm and unique contextual factors not familiar to health care professionals (Hanft & Striffler, 1995). Unfortunately, therapists' education about early intervention and school system practices tends to occur on the job rather than in the classroom (Hanft & Anzalone, 2001). New clinicians thus are faced with learning new skills for which they have little preparation or training. Even experienced professionals moving from a hospital setting will find the transition from a hospital to an educational culture to be overwhelming.

Another challenge to successful role release is competition among the professions. This is more common in occupational therapy, physical therapy, and speech-language pathology, due to such ongoing issues as therapists' fees and the restructuring of state laws that specify the kinds of care these disciplines are expected to deliver. Third-party reimbursement guidelines are increasingly restrictive as the costs of health care rise, and mandate

1. Team mission statement

2. Open and honest communication

3. Familiarity among team members

4. Family-centeredness

5. Team leadership/coordination

6. Support for one another

Table 2.1

documentation of discipline-specific information (Hanft & Anzalone, 2001). Also, local school budgets are stretched, often forcing administrators to limit services and increasing the competition among professions, especially when contractual occupational and physical therapy service providers are employed to fill the needs of early intervention/early childhood special education programs. Competing for funds can make it difficult for team members

The Process of Role Release

Role Release Component	Activities
Role Extension	• Read new articles and books within your discipline or about your child's condition. • Attend conferences, seminars, and lectures. • Join a professional organization in your field or a family-to-family network. • Explore resources at libraries or media centers.
Role Enrichment	• Listen to parents discuss their child's strengths and needs. • Ask for explanations of unfamiliar technical language or jargon. • Do an appraisal of what you wish you knew more about and what you could teach others.
Role Expansion	• Watch someone from another discipline work with a child, and check your perception of what you observe. • Attend a workshop in another field that includes some "hands-on" practicum experiences. • Rotate the role of transdisciplinary arena assessment facilitator among all service providers on the team.
Role Exchange	• Allow yourself to be videotaped practicing a technique from another discipline; invite a team member from that discipline to review and critique the videotape with you. • Work side-by-side in the center-based program, demonstrating interventions to families and staff. • Suggest strategies for achieving an Individualized Family Service Plan (IFSP) or Individual Education Plan (IEP) outcome outside your own discipline; check your accuracy with other team members.
Role Release	• Do a self-appraisal: List new skills within your intervention repertoire that other team members have taught you. • Monitor the performance of the service providers on your child's IFSP team. • Present on the "whole" child at a clinical conference. • Accept responsibility for implementing, with the family, an entire IFSP/IEP.
Role Support	• Ask for help when you feel "stuck." • Offer help when you see a team member struggling with a complex intervention • Provide any intervention that only you can provide, but share the child's progress and any related interventions with the primary service provider and the family.

From: Adapted from McGonigel, M. J., Woodruff, G., & Roszmann-Millican, M. (1994). The transdisciplinary team: A model for family-centered early intervention. In L. J. Johnson, R. J. Gallagher, & M. J. Lamontagne (Eds.), *Meeting early intervention challenges: Issues from birth to three* (2nd ed., pp. 95-131). Baltimore: Paul H. Brookes. Reprinted with permission. Reprinted with permission.

Table 2.2

who are struggling to work together in a supportive relationship.

Service Delivery in Natural Environments. The goal of providing services in natural environments is intended to facilitate families' ability to integrate recommendations from early intervention/early childhood special education service personnel into their daily lives, underscoring the importance of family participation and collaboration in service delivery (Hanft & Pilkington, 2000). Some professionals, however, may be uncomfortable in natural environments. Hanft and Pilkington (2000) note that therapists, in particular, may be uncomfortable when the equipment and materials they are accustomed to in clinics or therapy rooms are not available to them. Childress (2004) points out that delivering services in natural environments enables educators and other service providers to work with families to make the most of the resources present in their homes and other natural environments and to suggest modifications or accommodations when necessary. This context also enables families to embed recommendations into their daily routines more easily, thus providing consistent enhancement of the child's development. Therapists and educators who are not comfortable with their skills and knowledge, and who use their profession to maintain a distance between themselves and families find natural environments particularly difficult to negotiate.

Family-centered Services. The Infants and Toddlers With Disabilities Program was originally established by amendments to the Individuals With Disabilities Education Act (IDEA) as Part H, later changed to Part C in subsequent amendments. One aspect of delivery of services in Part C of IDEA is the mandate for services to be family-centered. This requirement has produced challenges for professionals who are members of transdisciplinary teams, including: insufficient time, narrow emphasis on professional expertise, feelings of competition or superiority, concerns about being able to make a difference, focus on child-centered rather than family-centered care, lack of professional education regarding family-centered care, and limited agency resources for supporting such care (Hirschberg, 1996; Shannon, 2004).

Challenges to family-centered care, as described by family members, are as follows: a lack of knowledge, experience, or ability related to early intervention/early childhood special education; lack of respect or being treated as irrelevant by professionals; a desire for more services and resources; time constraints; lack of inclusion in planning and intervention; and poor service coordination (Miller & Hanft, 1998; Shannon, 2004). Such feelings and practices restrict the ability of professionals to build a strong, collaborative relationship with families and minimize opportunities for professionals and families to combine their unique perspectives for the benefit of the child (Miller & Hanft, 1998). At the same time, family members' motivation and willingness to work with the rest of the team are necessary. Too often, professionals interpret families' considerations of the multiple issues in their lives as disinterest in early intervention/early childhood special education services. Shannon (2004) pointed out how professionals were quick to label families as "unmotivated," without considering such factors as financial constraints, other children in the family, conflicts with work schedules, and early intervention/education service provision. He also discussed the impact of personality traits on service delivery—assertive families are more likely to receive the care they seek, while passive or timid families do not. Westby and Ford (1993) noted that families from different cultures respond to the diagnosis of a disability differently, and that their response to the diagnosis, in turn, has an impact on their ability to participate in early intervention education services.

Culturally Appropriate Practices. According to Chen, Brekken, and Chan (1997), cultural competence is reflected by three characteristics: "(a) a person's self-awareness of their personal culture, values, and beliefs; (b) the knowledge of and respect for different cultures; and (c) skills in interacting and responding to individuals from other cultures" (p. 61). Professionals in early intervention/education programs should be comfortable when dealing with families from other cultures and be able to demonstrate cultural competence. Such families provide special challenges; their communication styles, cultural practices, and traditions may differ from those of a society's mainstream. Thus, team members must be flexible. When cultural norms differ, it is important for team members to avoid reacting critically to these differences. Families from other countries face difficulties inherent in trying to negotiate a new society where the rules and norms are unfamiliar to them. Not only must they learn about the practices within their community, just like any family would have to do, they also must learn about the practices associated with the services needed for children with disabilities.

Alvarado (2004) illustrates the impact of such efforts on two families who were undocumented Mexicans living in the United States and dealing with early intervention/education for their children with disabilities. While both families were concerned with the needs of their children, the day-to-day stresses of paying bills and negotiating a new society clearly took a toll.

Westby and Ford (1993) also point out how the culture(s) of a team affects the participation of a family on a team. This is an issue rarely recognized by teams, although such teams are quick to note the obstacles presented by a family's culture on early intervention/education services. Teams need to reflect on their own behavioral norms and expectations and how they may have an impact on families' willingness to participate.

Team Conflicts

No team can exist over a period of time without some disagreement or conflict. Cox (2003) defines conflict as "a clash or struggle that occurs when a real or perceived threat or difference exists in the desires, thoughts, attitudes, feelings or behaviors of two or more parties" (p. 154). Alternatively, Sessa, Bennett, and Birdsall (1993) define conflict as "a verbalization of differences" (p. 58). Different sources of conflict can exist—intrapersonal, intergroup, intragroup, and interorganizational. Conflicts around team tasks are less likely to be focused on personal issues, making them easier to negotiate. When conflicts become personal, they are more divisive and likely to have a particularly negative effect on the team. Sessa et al. (1993) indicate that team conflicts can result in growth and that the challenge is not avoiding conflict, but rather reducing stress resulting from conflict.

Potential Sources of Conflict. Intrapersonal and intergroup stress result from a variety of factors. As mentioned previously, the functions of the team can result in conflict. This kind of conflict is more likely to enable team members to remain neutral, because they understand that the source of the conflict is not personal (Sessa et al., 1993). Depersonalized conflict causes less distress for team members. One way to help team members be able to distance themselves from conflict is to understand that conflict creates the opportunity for the team to grow; thus, it should not be avoided. This kind of knowledge helps team members depersonalize disagreements and respond more positively when conflicts occur (Sessa et al., 1993).

Narrowly prescribed roles and a need to defend one's professional turf can limit team members' contributions, provide sources of disagreement, and create issues in service delivery and perception of status (Carpenter, King-Sears, & Keys, 1998; Hinojosa et al., 2001; Reese & Sontag, 2002). Team members may have limited perceptions or faulty knowledge regarding each other's roles and training—problems that result in part because related service professionals and teachers traditionally have been trained in isolation from each other. Hinojosa et al. (2001) describe a case in which therapists, despite making no effort to learn about the educational setting, assumed that teachers would carry out their recommendations and practiced pullout interventions rather than integrating their services into the classroom.

Another related source of conflict is role blurring. Various professions have overlapping roles—for example, occupational and physical therapy. Role blurring can cause competition and decreased quality of service. For example, clinicians' refusal to share information or participate in group activities can alienate members from each other and ultimately influence the services provided and the manner in which they are delivered (Reese & Sontag, 2002). One of the most unfortunate situations is when families are caught in conflicts between other team members. Instead of only dealing with the stresses around their child's disability, family members have the added tension of trying to interact with team members who give conflicting advice and are palpably hostile to each other.

Dettmer, Thurston, and Dyck (2002) discuss resistance to change as another source of conflict. They note that professionals are often vested in maintaining the status quo and are reluctant to change familiar practices. Change means unknown consequences, and professionals may be uncomfortable with the unclear path of new programs. Some people have a low tolerance for change, especially when it results in the need to learn new ways of dealing with job responsibilities. Professionals who are new to their field and are still forging their identity can be particularly threatened by the need to change.

Intragroup conflicts can arise from intrapersonal issues (Cox, 2003), such as lack of commitment to the team process due to personal agendas, lack of willingness to share equally in the team's work, refusal to accept responsibility for one's own actions, and individual perception of status among team members. As mentioned earlier, these behaviors are harder to deal with than team process conflicts. Consider Ogletree's (2001) characteristics of good teams (see Table 2.1). Support, honest communication, and familiarity are not easily developed when one or more team members refuse to work and will not accept ownership for their behavior. Unless all members of the team have common goals and are willing to work for them, the team will become unbalanced and be in a continuous state of conflict.

Limiting Team Conflict. The inevitability of conflict highlights the need for teams to plan strategies in advance for dealing with the issues. Dettmer et al. (2002) discussed personal strategies for individuals to use when dealing with conflict that have application to this discussion as well. Some suggested strategies to help limit and manage conflicts include the education of all team members regarding the other members' training and roles. As noted earlier, most professions educate students according to strict criteria by national accrediting agencies, leaving little opportunity for learning about other disciplines. Learning more about others on the team prepares members for the kind of input to expect. It also can help team members understand the different professional challenges each discipline faces. Along the same lines, eliminating or minimizing the use of discipline-specific jargon helps decrease defensiveness and facilitate communication.

Establishing procedures for team members to give and receive feedback to one another in a nonthreatening way is an additional method for depersonalizing conflicts (Reese & Sontag, 2002). This is particularly true when conflicts arise over turf issues and professional roles. Working as a team evolves as a process—learning to respond positively to questions often is related to how the question is asked. Having team members practice how to ask questions in a nonthreatening manner can help teams to respond rather than react, resulting in constructive dialogue. One example here would be a discussion regarding the benefits of the coordinated, collaborative approach, which is the aim of transdisciplinary teams. Keeping in mind your tone of voice and the manner in which you ask questions is a good way to practice giving and receiving feedback in a positive way.

Periodic review of team values, missions, and processes serves to reconnect team members to the purpose of the team. It also serves to ensure that team members understand aspects of team structure and function, including behavioral norms, rules of conduct, and decision making. During such reviews, it is important that all team members feel they have an equal opportunity to be heard. Setting time limits in advance on how long people can talk and then enforcing those time limits helps such sessions to be as effective and efficient as possible. Identifying areas where changes to function and structure are needed is important so that teams can grow and adjust, as circumstances require.

Managing Anger and Negativity. Dettmer et al. (2002) describe the push-push back phenomenon that occurs during conflict. This kind of event occurs when a person responds angrily, or "pushes," and the person to whom this response is directed reacts by "pushing back." It is important for people involved in these kinds of exchanges to manage their reactions to negative input and not push back, thus preventing the conflict from escalating. Dettmer et al. (2002) discuss postponing reactions to negative comments, being quiet, and listening. Doing so requires effort and commitment. It is not easy to listen when one is feeling attacked; however, reacting in a knee-jerk fashion only escalates the situation. It is necessary to stand back from the situation and try to observe events from afar, which can detach group members from their feelings of anger and help to separate the person from the issues at hand.

A final step for managing personal conflicts is taking time to respond to feelings once the conflict is over. The group needs to deal with members' resistance, defensiveness, and anger before problem solving can begin. Setting time aside to deal with feelings after an event, rather than burying them, is healthy. Acknowledging feelings does not change them, but does diminish the power they have to thwart group processes.

Conclusion

Given the challenges that transdisciplinary teams often face, can they be successful in providing services? The answer is a resounding yes. The key to an effective team is awareness beforehand that everyone needs to demonstrate commitment, patience, creativity, and a sense of humor. The systems in which teams work often do more to get in their way than to facilitate the tasks with which they are charged. Those of us who make up teams are the only ones who can ensure their success. In the process, they can grow, learn, and develop a great sense of satisfaction in the work they have chosen to do.

References

Alvarado, M. I. (2004). Mucho camino: The experiences of two undocumented Mexican mothers participating in their child's early intervention program. *American Journal of Occupational Therapy, 58*, 521-530.

Bens, I. (1999, July/August). Keeping your team out of trouble. [Electronic version]. *The Journal for Quality and Participation,* 45-47.

Carpenter, S., King-Sears, M., & Keys, S. G. (1998). Counselors + educators + families as a transdisciplinary team = more effective inclusion for students with disabilities. *Professional School Counseling, 2*(1), 1-10.

Chen, D., Brekken, L. J., & Chan, S. (1997). Project CRAFT: Culturally responsive and family-focused training. *Infants and Young Children, 10*(1), 61-73.

Childress, D. C. (2004). Special instruction and natural environments: Best practices in early intervention. *Infants and Young Children, 17,* 162-170.

Cox, K. B. (2003). The effects of intrapersonal, intragroup, and intergroup conflict on team performance effectiveness and job satisfaction. *Nursing Administration Quarterly, 27*(2), 153-163.

Dettmer, P., Thurston, C. P., & Dyck, N. (2002). *Consultation, collaboration, and teamwork for students with special needs.* Boston: Allyn & Bacon.

Galentine, J. K., & Seery, M. E. (1999). Achieving role expansion and release: Conversation strategies used by one transdisciplinary team. *Infant-Toddler Intervention: The Transdisciplinary Journal, 9*(1), 17-38.

Hanft, B., & Anzalone, M. (2001). Issues in professional development: Preparing and supporting occupational therapists in early childhood. *Infants and Young Children, 13,* 67-78.

Hanft, B., & Pilkington, K. O. (2000). Therapy in natural environments: The means of end goal for early intervention. *Infants and Young Children, 12,* 1-12.

Hanft, B., & Striffler, N. (1995). Incorporating developmental therapy in early childhood programs: Challenges and promising practices. *Infants and Young Children, 8,* 37-47.

Hinojosa, J., Bedell, G., Buchholz, E., Charles, J., Shigaki, I., & Bicchieri, S. (2001). Team collaboration: A case study of an early intervention team. *Qualitative Health Research, 11,* 206-220.

Hirschberg, L. M. (1996). History-making, not history-taking: Clinical interviews with infants and their families. In S. J. Meisels & E. Fenichel (Eds.), *New visions for the developmental assessment of infants and young children* (pp. 85-124). Washington, DC: Zero to Three, National Center for Infants, Toddlers, and Families.

Individuals With Disabilities Education Improvement Act, 20 U.S.C. §602 (2004).

McEwen, I., & Shelden, M. L. (1995). Pediatric therapy in the 1990s: The demise of the educational versus medical dichotomy. *Physical and Occupational Therapy in Pediatrics, 15,* 33-45.

McGonigel, M. J., Woodruff, G., & Roszmann-Millican, M. (1994). The transdisciplinary team: A model for family-centered early intervention. In L. J. Johnson, R. J. Gallagher, & M. J. Lamontagne (Eds.), *Meeting early intervention challenges: Issues from birth to three* (2nd ed., pp. 95-131). Baltimore: Paul H. Brookes.

Miller, L. J., & Hanft, B. (1998). Building positive alliances: Partnerships with families as the cornerstone of developmental assessment. *Infants and Young Children, 11,* 49-60.

Ogletree, B. T. (2001). Team-based delivery for students with disabilities. *Intervention in School & Clinics, 36*(3), 138-146.

Reese, D. J., & Sontag, M. (2002). Successful interprofessional collaboration on the hospice team. *Health and Social Work, 26*(3), 167-175.

Rothermich, A. E., Kinnear, C. L., & Beck, S. L. (1996). From unpleasant surprises to productive relationships: Becoming team builders. *Hospital Topics, 53*(13), 1565-1569.

Sessa, V. I., Bennett, J., & Birdsall, C. (1993). Conflict with less distress: Promoting team effectiveness. *Nursing Administration Quarterly, 18*(1), 57-65.

Shannon, P. (2004). Barriers to family-centered services for infants and toddlers with developmental delays. *Social Work, 49,* 301-308.

Westby, C. E., & Ford, V. (1993). The role of team culture in assessment and intervention. *Journal of Educational and Psychological Consultation, 4,* 319-341.

Chapter 3

Case Study:
The Gonzales Family

The following case study illustrates the value of adopting a family-based approach in early intervention/education, as well as the challenges and opportunities of participating as transdisciplinary team members. It is important to remember that all families are different and vary across a number of dimensions that shape their cultural identity, including race, ethnicity, religion, geographical location, income status, gender, disability status, and occupation. In this case, the family is described in terms of various cultural dimensions, as well as their unique experiences and their vision for the future of their young child with a disability.

The Gonzales Family

The Gonzales family includes Roberto and Francisca Gonzales and their children—8-year-old Roberto, 6-year-old Maria, 5-year-old Javier, and 3-year-old Luis. The family moved from Mexico to the United States seven years ago in search of work and a better life. They have lived in a rural area in the southeastern United States over the past six years and are undocumented immigrants. Mr. Gonzales' parents have lived with them for three years and help care for the children. Since Maria, Javier, and Luis were born in the United States, they are considered United States citizens.

As an undocumented immigrant, Mr. Gonzales is unable to qualify for a regular job. He waits daily in a location known as a pick-up spot for undocumented immigrant men who are looking for work that pays "under the table." Here, groups of men wait to be selected for work in construction or landscaping on a day-to-day basis. Mrs. Gonzales takes care of their home and children with assistance from the grandparents, particularly the grandmother.

The Gonzales family lives in a large, three-bedroom mobile home in a community that has seen a steady increase in the Hispanic population. The family members are close with one another and enjoy spending time together. In addition, they have a small circle of close friends in the community. They are committed and active members of a small Catholic church in their area, which has a strong Hispanic ministry.

The two oldest children attend the neighborhood elementary school; the family is considering enrolling Javier there as well. Roberto learned English in school and is helping Maria and Javier learn the language. Although Maria's academic difficulties initially had been attributed to English being her second language, she recently was referred for an evaluation for a suspected learning disability because her academic problems have worsened. Mrs. Gonzales and the grandparents do not speak English, and so Roberto translates for them. Mr. Gonzales translates when he can, but is unable to be away from his day-to-day work situation very often. He has chosen a good friend to translate when he is unavailable.

The three youngest children have medical coverage through the state Medicaid program and receive services through the county health clinic. Because he needs to work, Mr. Gonzales rarely is able to drive the family to doctor visits at the local health department. The close circle of four friends, well-known to the Gonzales family, use the car to transport the family to the clinic and other meetings when Mr. Gonzales cannot attend. These friends share the expenses of the vehicle.

Aside from Maria, Javier, and Luis, no other family members are covered by health insurance, due to their undocumented immigrant status. The family's health care expenses are significant as they are committed to finding a cure for Javier, who has serious health problems. The idea for a cure came about as a result of the family's involvement with their church. They plan to participate in a pilgrimage to the Basilica of Guadalupe in Mexico City. The family will take two trips to the Basilica. One trip will be to make a pledge to walk from the entrance of the basilica to the altar on their knees if Javier is cured. If he is cured, they will make a second trip to carry out this promise. In order to make this trip, the entire family has been working at whatever jobs they can find and putting aside funds to pay for the trip and associated expenses.

Javier

Javier is an outgoing 5-year-old boy who has thoracic spina bifida (thoracic myelomeningocele) and hydrocephalus, which was shunted soon after birth. Since the initial shunt placement, Javier has had several shunt infections that required surgery. Unable to walk, Javier has a manual wheelchair that he uses to get around at school. In addition to using the wheelchair, Javier also uses a dynamic stander, forearm crutches, and leg braces. At home, he usually moves around by pulling himself across the floor or is carried by family members, a method they prefer over his use of the wheelchair, both at home and in the community.

Javier loves playing outside with his sister, brothers, and neighborhood friends. He enjoys watching *Sesame Street* (Elmo is his favorite character) and moving in time to music, especially when his brothers turn up the volume on the radio. Some of Javier's other favorite activities include looking at books and being read to, as long as the stories are short and simple.

Javier is able to self-propel his wheelchair for distances up to 10 feet on level surfaces at school, but he requires a great deal of assistance from his teachers to transfer in and out of his chair. His mother and grandmother, who provide his care, are hesitant to learn transfer techniques, since they do not use the wheelchair at home. The therapists who work with Javier have noticed that while the family will agree to their recommendations, they do not appear to actually carry them out at home.

Javier has recurrent temper tantrums, which result when he does not get what he wants, such as his siblings' toys or attention. On rare occasions, Roberto, Maria, or Luis will have similar outbursts, for which they are severely disciplined by Mrs. Gonzales or the grandmother. They do not punish Javier similarly—he is excused as a "poor thing" who lives a "horrible life." Roberto, Maria, and Luis do not understand why Javier is not punished for the same behaviors that earn them quick and severe reprimands. The management of Javier's behavior has become a major issue for the Gonzales family.

Javier does not talk at the same level of most of his age-mates (in Spanish or English). He speaks short sentences in Spanish, mostly 3- to 4-words long, but does not use longer sentences and cannot carry on a conversation in his native language. Javier speaks a number of words in English, but he knows only a few English phrases. Sometimes he has a difficult time understanding what his family and neighborhood friends say to him (again, in Spanish or English), so others have learned to sometimes use gestures to aid his comprehension. The family speaks for Javier when he is communicating with people outside of their immediate circle. Recently, Javier was diagnosed with a mild hearing loss in his right ear and a mild to moderate loss in his left ear (which helps to explain some of his communication difficulties), so he will be using hearing aids.

Various aspects of self-care, such as dressing and toileting, are difficult for Javier. His mother and grandmother put on and remove his clothing (e.g., jacket, pants, shoes, socks, rain gear, hat). His family worries about his health and makes sure he is protected from the weather. Javier's mother and grandmother often assist with other aspects self-care, such as feeding him and wiping his face and blowing his nose. Roberto and Maria also help take care of both Javier and Luis, something the family counts on in certain settings, such as at school. In addition, Javier does not have bladder or bowel control. As a result, his bladder is catheterized every 4 hours and he wears a diaper.

Mr. Gonzales remains emotionally distant from all the children. This is especially true for Javier, whose disability Mr. Gonzales sees as a negative reflection on his manhood. As a result, Mr. Gonzales leaves all of Javier's care to Mrs. Gonzales and the grandmother.

On a regular basis, Javier is taken to an urban area in an adjacent county an hour away to attend a spina bifida clinic provided by the state rehabilitation agency for children with special health care needs. It is here that he has begun receiving audiological services for his newly diagnosed hearing loss.

Early Intervention and Preschool Services

As a toddler, Javier and his family received a wide range of services through the state's Part C Early Intervention System. Weekly home-based services were provided through a collaborative transdisciplinary team model, where one or two professionals served as the primary service providers and professionals from other disciplines provided consultation regarding goal development, skill development, family support, etc. The physical therapist initially served as the primary provider, with the speech-language pathologist and occupational therapist serving in secondary roles. Over time, the early childhood special educator provided special instruction and served as the primary provider, with the other disciplines serving in secondary roles. Service coordination, provided by a social worker, was an integral part of services throughout Javier's time in early intervention. When communication needs could not be met through a Spanish-speaking service provider or through family friends who spoke English, the early intervention program provided interpreter services.

The Gonzales family presented some challenges that the early intervention program staff had difficulty addressing. The family seemed to be overwhelmed and confused due to their lack of familiarity with many of the systems (e.g., health, education) in the United States and how they operated, particularly early intervention services. Because the Gonzales family was unfamiliar with the early intervention system and seemed to be unsure of how it operated, they constantly asked questions about what services to expect. At the prompting of Mrs. Gonzales, Mr. Gonzales and a neighbor who spoke some English made repeated phone calls to each member of the team, asking the same questions repeatedly. Although the early intervention program staff wanted to be as helpful as possible to the family, they became frustrated when the family seemed to question them so much.

Another problem for the staff was that the Gonzales family was constantly late for meetings, and sometimes not at home when service providers arrived for scheduled visits. Mrs. Gonzales insisted on serving food when she was available, and tended to talk about many things other than Javier during the early part of each visit. This often meant that visits lasted considerably longer than planned and home visits to other families in the program suffered as a result. At the same time, the team members were aware that this family felt great responsibility for Javier's disability and suffered from guilt and shame that led to continuing depression. Thus, many of the team members struggled with how to provide the support needed by the Gonzales family.

Early on, Javier's parents identified several family strengths, which included their close ties to their community and the amount of support that they received from close friends. The Gonzales family wanted Javier to attend the local Head Start program when he was age 3. His older siblings and many of their neighbors' children had attended this program and the Gonzaleses were pleased with the program. The early intervention team supported the Head Start placement and facilitated Javier's transition to the program, which was located in a building adjacent to the neighborhood school (4 miles from the family's home).

When he turned 3, Javier began attending the Head Start preschool program daily for four hours a day. A family friend, whose children also attended the program, used the Gonzales family car to transport Javier to Head Start along with her own children. A collaborative relationship developed between the Head Start program and the local school system. The school system provided related services for the program's eligible children with disabilities. The Head Start program, in turn, provided an inclusive educational setting, in which eligible 3- and 4-year-olds with disabilities had access to preschool experiences with typical peers. This particular Head Start program also employed a specialist out of the regional office who provided periodic support and technical assistance to Head Start programs in the southeast, which served other children from Hispanic communities.

While attending Head Start, Javier's frequent temper tantrums presented special difficulties, especially since his mother and grandmother saw no reason to intervene with these tantrums at home and disagreed with the teachers' methods of managing the behavior. Over time, the teachers were able to explain to the family why they needed to limit Javier's tantrums at school, although this did not change the family's behavior at home.

Javier received weekly services from an early childhood special education teacher and speech-language pathologist. Occupational therapy and physical therapy consultations were provided on a monthly basis, the focus being to get Javier accustomed to using his wheelchair in the Head Start environment. These services were all provided at the Head Start program; Javier's teachers, one who spoke some Spanish, had the support of these professionals. Bladder care was not an issue because he was only in the program for half a day.

A lack of understanding regarding the family's cultural practices was apparent as the team members interacted with the Gonzales family. Javier's team struggled with several issues that caused problems between the family and professionals. All of the therapists had concerns that the family did not follow through on the team's recommendations in the home environment. This concern was exacerbated by the fact that the family was consistently either late for, or missed, team meetings. Some of the early intervention team members found it difficult to be positive about the planned pilgrimage to Mexico City, something the family discussed constantly. Some of the team members did not understand why the family was engaging in this activity and questioned the usefulness of the pilgrimage. They were particularly concerned that Javier would not be receiving early intervention services during this time.

Transition to Kindergarten

During the winter of his last year in the Head Start program, the family and other team members began discussing his transition to elementary school. Figure 3.1 highlights the concerns expressed by the various participants present at a meeting held to discuss Javier's transition to kindergarten. The school system's special education coordinator encouraged the family to consider sending Javier to a newer school, located 25 miles from the Gonzales' home, that had a special education classroom. To support her recommendation, she highlighted the physical access, small class size, number of available therapists, and the presence of a full-time nurse to give Javier his medications and manage his catheterization.

Transition to Kindergarten Meeting (Winter)

Participants and Their Major Concerns/Issues

Mr. & Mrs. Gonzales
- Distance of new school from home
- Inability of the brother and sister to watch out for Javier
- Transportation/safety of Javier
- Uncertainty about the new staff and system

Head Start Teacher
- Distance of new school from home
- New school away from community of friends and siblings
- Javier would benefit from spending majority of day in kindergarten class rather than special education class
- Neighborhood school would provide continuity of same therapists
- Javier's tantrums and need to limit them at school
- Family tardiness at or missing planned meetings

Speech-Language Pathologist
- Kindergarten teachers in neighborhood school very familiar/experienced with teaching Spanish-speaking children
- Family education on hearing aid management and language facilitation

Physical Therapist
- Physical accessibility of neighborhood school building
- Transportation for either neighborhood school or new school
- Mobility within the school environment
- Lack of family follow-through

Occupational Therapist
- Physical accessibility of neighborhood school building
- Transportation for either neighborhood school or new school
- Self-care needs within the school environment
- Lack of family follow-through

Special Education Coordinator
- Physical accessibility of neighborhood school building
- Lack of special education class in neighborhood school
- Lack of full-time school nurse in neighborhood school

Neighborhood School Principal
- Cost of making school more accessible
- Cost of additional personnel to meet the needs of one child

Figure 3.1

Some team members objected to the special educator's assumption that Javier needed a self-contained placement and for imposing her views on the family. The family responded to these recommendations with suspicion, fearful that Javier was being purposefully separated from his siblings and that he would not be well-cared for if the transfer to the newer school went through. These concerns led Mr. Gonzales and the family friends to make a barrage of phone calls to the Head Start staff and the special education coordinator.

The neighborhood school building was over 50 years old, not accessible to someone with disabilities, and in need of repairs. Potential problems at the neighborhood school included physical barriers and space issues (e.g., kindergarten classrooms in trailers, few curbed ramps), a limited transportation schedule, and the lack of a true special education class. The school nurse was only available on a part-time basis. A location for the catheterization program and personnel to carry it out in the absence of the nurse would need to be identified. One potential advantage of the neighborhood school, however, would be that Javier would be placed in the general education kindergarten classroom. It would be the only placement choice for him, but would be the appropriate choice, based on his needs.

Ultimately, the decision was made that Javier would attend his neighborhood school. His parents were glad that he would be attending the same school as their other children, but expressed concerns about the danger of Javier riding the bus, other children making fun of him, or being asked to do things he was not able to do. It was apparent that a number of steps would have to be taken to address these concerns and to ease Javier's transition to the new school. Mrs. Gonzales and the grandmother offered to come to the school to assist with Javier's care—feeding him and performing other tasks as needed.

A series of observations and meetings were arranged to assess Javier's needs within the neighborhood school. Some of Javier's current interventionists, including his physical therapist and occupational therapist, conducted an ecological assessment of the school to determine what improvements would be needed to make the school more physically accessible for Javier. A plan was designed, with input from the family and personnel at the new school, to ensure physical accessibility in all aspects of the new environment.

One of the kindergarten teachers and the special education teachers visited the Head Start program. They were able to see that Javier, like many of his peers, was energetic and curious. He eagerly engaged in some of the classroom activities, appeared to follow adult direction, and was responsive to adult praise. Javier continued to have temper tantrums, however; the tantrums usually occurred when he was being asked to perform activities he felt he could not do or did not want to do. He selected activities in which he felt most competent, and often engaged in solitary play. The other children in the preschool clearly were very fond of Javier in spite of his tantrums, and they were all quick to help him with any task—sometimes doing too much for him.

Javier learned his colors and shapes while in preschool and began to use a few more words in English. Mild cognitive delays were observed, especially in the area of reasoning and problem solving in more abstract situations. Other challenges included fine-motor activities, such as object assembly (e.g., Legos or blocks), snipping with scissors, and copying shapes using a pencil or crayon, all of which were issues of concern for his teachers and occupational therapist.

IEP Development

Two IEP meetings were held in the spring, attended by the family, Head Start staff, and school system representatives. By this time, the school system personnel had begun to realize that Mr. Gonzales was frequently late for the meetings and that he would not make decisions at first meetings. Accordingly, two meetings were planned. For the first meeting, the team discussed and began to develop a plan for the coming year, putting their recommendations in writing (this was then translated into Spanish). Mr. Gonzales was late to the meeting and the team meeting started later than planned; therefore, the meeting ran late and one of the team members had to leave before the meeting was over because she couldn't stay past the planned time. This team member submitted her concerns and suggestions for goals in writing so that the team could discuss them during the meeting. Observations and results of formal and informal testing were shared. The overall team goals for Javier for the coming school year were discussed, with input provided by Mr. Gonzales about the family's desires and priorities. Mr. Gonzales then took this information home to discuss with his family. Later, a second meeting was scheduled to discuss the family's questions, determine their satisfaction with the plan, and inquire about any additions or changes. Strengths and needs were identified and discussed. Figure 3.2 highlights the participants of the IEP meeting and the areas of concern.

Discussion: Issues/Team Strategies

The team must deal with many issues in their efforts to meet Javier's needs in the new school environment. These involve cultural, religious, parenting/caretaking, and educational/behavioral issues, all of which have implications in terms of developing and implementing an individualized education plan. Table 3.1 summarizes the issues and strategies.

Issue: The family is frequently tardy for meetings. This is a cultural issue rather than a lack of concern or rudeness on the part of the family, which the team members need to understand.

Strategy: When setting appointments for meetings, the family should be scheduled to come early and the team should plan to be at the meeting later (15-20 minutes, depending on the usual length of tardiness that has been observed in past meetings). If time continues to be an issue for the team, one team member can be designated to stay throughout the meeting if other members must leave.

Issue: The Gonzaleses make many phone calls to various team members, whereby they ask the same questions repeatedly. This issue may stem in part from the family's lack of familiarity with the early intervention system and their cautious behavior resulting from their need to "operate outside the system" as undocumented immigrants. However, it also shows how concerned they are about Javier and the services he receives.

Strategy: The team will designate one member to have responsibility for responding to the family's phone calls. When an individual team member receives a call or a message to return a call, they will respond with, "The team will get back to you about this issue." The team will confer frequently regarding the phone requests and provide a message/response, delivered by one member of the team only. This will help to provide clarity and consistency for the Gonzales family and supply them with the information that they want and need.

Issue: Members of the team are very concerned about the family's reluctance to discipline Javier and their heightened vigilance to protect him from physical and emotional injury. The family's concerns are not only those familiar to many parents, they also have concerns rooted in the family's culture. While the therapists and other team members may feel that the family is "babying" Javier, as they are reluctant to encourage his independence, the team will need to acknowledge these family behaviors and concerns as a part of their cultural heritage.

Strategy: While the therapists and teachers may value children's independent mobility and self-care skills at an early age, any attempts to push for Javier's independence early on may result in alienating the family and jeopardizing collaboration between the family and the other team members. The therapists will need to consider compromising in terms of pushing the family to promote independent wheelchair mobility at home and in the community. The family values being able to take care of Javier themselves and they feel that the use of a wheelchair at home and in the community will highlight the fact that Javier is "different" and may give the appearance that they are not able to take care of him. At Javier's current age and size, carrying him is not a problem. As he grows older and becomes too big to handle, however, the family may be ready to consider wheelchair usage outside the school environment. The therapists will focus on the use of the wheelchair and other equipment in the school environment and should plant seeds concerning its *future* use in the home and community.

Issue: The family is committed to achieving a cure for Javier through a religious pilgrim-

---

Individual Education Plan Meeting (Spring)

Participants and Areas of Concern

Mr. & Mrs. Gonzales
- Transportation/safety of Javier
- Other children making fun of Javier
- Javier being pushed to do things he is unable to do
- Concern about management of temper tantrums

Head Start Teacher
- Participation primarily as support for family and to facilitate communication regarding Javier's current level of skills
- Management of temper tantrums
- Inconsistent attendance by the family at meetings

Kindergarten Teacher
- Pre-academic, cognitive, and early literacy skills
- Mobility within the classroom to get to various learning centers
- Positioning and use of other special seating/equipment
- Hygiene/toileting needs
- Safety

Early Childhood Special Education Teacher
- Participation primarily as support for kindergarten teacher in order to facilitate Javier's inclusion in the kindergarten class

Speech-Language Pathologist
- Attention, listening, comprehension, and language skills
- Communication

Physical Therapist
- Transportation to and from school
- Use of wheelchair and mobility within the school environment
- Transfers

Occupational Therapist
- Self-care skills for dressing, feeding, and toileting
- Hygiene skills
- Hand skills—delays in pre-writing skills

School Nurse
- Health care plan development
- Safety

Figure 3.2

Issues and Strategies for Addressing Them

ISSUE	STRATEGY
Tardiness for team meetings ⊙ Family has history of being late for scheduled meetings/conferences or not being prepared or available when a home visit was scheduled	⊙ Acknowledge tardiness is likely to continue ⊙ Structure meeting times to accommodate for tardiness
Constant phone calls ⊙ Same questions asked repeatedly	⊙ Develop team response to questions ⊙ Designate single member of team to respond to phone calls
Mobility issues ⊙ Family wants to carry Javier at home and in community rather than use his wheelchair ⊙ Therapists want to see Javier become more independent, with mobility in all environments	⊙ Work on mobility skills/independence in the school environment ⊙ Don't force use of wheelchair/mobility aids at home, rather look for opportunities to suggest when use of wheelchair might be helpful to family at home
Pilgrimage ⊙ Family is committed to making pilgrimage for a cure, which would take Javier away from needed services	⊙ Acknowledge family's belief and commitment ⊙ Suggest strategies to use while the family is on the pilgrimage
Management of tantrums ⊙ Family sees behavior as natural response to disability; they believe that Javier requires comfort, rather than discipline	⊙ Positive feedback and rewards for appropriate responses ⊙ Time out for tantrum behavior ⊙ Sensitize class members to Javier's behavior/responses
Parent care at school ⊙ Mother and grandmother want to come to school to take care of Javier	⊙ Encourage mother or grandmother to be at school ⊙ Team members utilize these days to be available for parent instruction and encouragement of carryover into home environment

Table 3.1

age. This commitment is supported by the family's church. This intention has the potential of devaluing the goals for Javier to become more independent in his mobility and self-care abilities at school, as well as take time away from the services he needs. In addition, the sacrifices that the family will make to be able to carry out a pilgrimage will negatively affect their financial well-being, placing them under additional stress.

Strategy: While the team may not share the family's belief in or commitment to making the pilgrimage, it is important that the team members be respectful and accepting of the family's desire and plans. Conveying respect will make it more likely that the family will be receptive to interventions for Javier in the interim while the family is planning for the pilgrimage.

Issue: Mrs. Gonzales and the grandmother want to come to school to take care of Javier on an ongoing basis. Some members of the team believe that this decision reflects the family's uncertainty toward the school staff regarding their ability to care for Javier, especially in light of the fact that the family does not support the goals targeting Javier's independent self-care skills and managing his tantrums. At the same time, the team members see the presence of the family at school on some regular basis as an opportunity for collaboration and informa-tion exchange.

Strategy: The team decided that either Mrs. Gonzales or the grandmother would attend school on a regular basis for full days, arriving with the neighbor who drives Javier to school and leaving with him when he is picked up at the end of the school day. A translator will be present on the days that the family attends. During their time at school, they will assist by encouraging Javier to push his wheelchair and helping the nurse with his catheterization program. Other team members will arrange to be available on those days. The occupa-tional therapist will be present during lunch to discuss Javier's progress in self-feeding and simple hygiene tasks and to point out why such skills are important to have at school. The physical therapist will demonstrate changes in Javier's mobility skills and strength, and the speech-language pathologist will engage the family in his communication intervention and discuss improvements. All of the related service personnel will tactfully suggest how the same skills easily could be infused into the ongoing activities that occur at home and in the community.

Issue: Tantrum management is a particularly sensitive area for the family. They believe it is their role to care for Javier's special needs and make his life easier. Javier's tantrums are seen as his response to his disability, requiring comfort from the family, rather than discipline. The other team members have a different perspective, seeing the tantrums as Javier's method of manipulating situations.

Strategy: During IEP planning meetings, the team gently but persistently described strat-egies to manage Javier's tantrums. Javier would be rewarded and given positive feedback when performing tasks asked of him. If he threw a tantrum, the team would give Javier time to cool off and encourage him to cease his behavior, then put him into time out. For the sake of consistency, classmates and team members would be instructed in responding appropriately.

As mentioned earlier, these positive behavioral support strategies were a source of po-tential conflict when family members spent the day at school. On the other hand, having Mrs. Gonzales in the classroom was a way to build trust between the family and the school. The team hoped that, with time, Javier's progress would be a source of pride to the family. Furthermore, they hoped that by observing at school, the family would begin to see that the disruption resulting from his tantrums should not be allowed to continue.

The decision to encourage the family to come to the school on a regular basis meant extra effort and potential dissension. However, the team chose this strategy in the hope that doing so would build trust over time and help the family become more committed to a long-term plan for Javier, through which his full potential could be realized.

Chapter 4

What Others Should Know About Early Childhood Special Educators

Jennifer L. Kilgo

As emphasized throughout this book, the field of early intervention/early childhood special education (EI/ECSE) is an evolving one that spans the birth through 8 age range and includes early intervention, preschool special education, and early primary special education. Just as the EI/ECSE field has evolved, so have the job requirements of the early childhood special educator, who may assume various professional responsibilities. These responsibilities were derived from the purposes of EI/ECSE, as outlined and supported in the Individuals With Disabilities Education Improvement Act (IDEA) (2004). Early childhood special educators may work directly with infants and young children with special needs, as well as in a collaborative relationship with general early childhood educators, family members, and related service professionals serving young children with special needs. They may assume positions in early intervention programs, hospital settings, ECSE classrooms, Head Start, and inclusive early childhood and early primary settings in both public and private schools, specialized agencies, or other settings where young children with known or suspected disabilities and their families receive services (Miller & Stayton, 2005). They may be known by one or more of the following job titles: early interventionist, early childhood special education teacher, inclusion specialist, service coordinator, consulting teacher, and family liaison, among others.

Educational Preparation of the Early Childhood Special Educator

Those professionals seeking degrees in early childhood special education will be prepared to work with young children with disabilities and their families. The age ranges of the children will vary from birth to 5 years, birth to 8 years, or ages 3 through 8, depending on the certifications being offered. Early childhood special educators may obtain degrees at the bachelor's, master's, and doctoral levels.

Direction and guidance for determining the competence of early childhood special educators comes from the primary professional organization that represents this discipline, the Division for Early Childhood (DEC) of the Council for Exceptional Children (CEC). Early childhood special educators acquire content knowledge and skills as specified by DEC and CEC, which offer a set of knowledge and skill standards that reflect what ECSE teachers should know and be able to do to work effectively with young children with known or suspected disabilities (Stayton, Miller, & Dinnebeil, 2003). The educational requirements and curricula for ECSE personnel preparation programs are grounded in research-based practices for young children with disabilities, their families, and the personnel who work on their behalf. Additional guidance to the preparation of early childhood special educators can be found in the recommended practice guidelines developed by DEC, which are based on scientific review of the research literature (over 1,000 articles were reviewed)

special education

showing positive outcomes for children and/or families (Sandall, Hemmeter, Smith, & McLean, 2005).

Early childhood special educators must possess a broad array of skills across multiple content areas in order to effectively serve young children with disabilities and their families. They require a common core of knowledge and skills necessary to work with young children experiencing typical development, as well as specialized knowledge and skills regarding young children with special needs and their families. Because of the expanded number of inclusive early childhood programs, early childhood special educators often work with children without disabilities, as well. The philosophy of ECSE is that learning environments, instructional practices, and other components of programs designed for young children with special needs should be based on what is typically expected of, and experienced by, children of different ages and developmental stages. Programs for children with disabilities may require additional individualized goals and specialized interventions to be applied, as needed, in order to provide the necessary services for these children.

The educational programs for early childhood special educators most often include classes in providing family-based services, conducting comprehensive assessments, developing and implementing intervention plans and strategies, participating on teams, coordinating services for families, and serving as an advocate for children and families (Kilgo & Bruder, 1997). In addition to acquiring the content knowledge, early childhood special educators must have appropriate field experiences during which they apply this content. Thus, early childhood special educators are prepared to promote child engagement, independence, and mastery; support children and families in achieving their individual goals; promote development in all important domains; build and support social competence; facilitate the generalized use of skills; prepare children for normalized life experiences with their families in their programs/schools and in their communities; help children and their families make smooth transitions; and prevent or minimize the development of future problems or disabilities.

Roles and Contributions of the Early Childhood Special Educator on the Team

The early childhood special educator may work directly with children with various types of delays and disabilities, as well as with adult family members and professionals from other disciplines. Because the early childhood special educator's role on the team cuts across developmental areas and has an important link to all of the related service areas, it is imperative for the early childhood special educator to be adequately prepared to assume the responsibilities associated with this role. Furthermore, it is essential that professionals from other disciplines understand the responsibilities and roles of early childhood special educators and be willing to work collaboratively with them on the team. In center- or school-based settings, the ECSE teacher serves as the central point of contact on the team and is sometimes a liaison between the family and other team members on a day-to-day basis. In home-based programs, the early childhood special educator may provide service coordination and direct instruction within the natural environment, as well as consultation and support to families or other care providers.

Early childhood special educators need to have a broad conceptual knowledge base of developmental processes and curricular domains in order to address the overall needs of young children. This broad conceptual base allows for flexibility in adapting for children with special needs. Early childhood special educators actively seek input from other professionals and coordinate this information for conducting assessments and planning programs and service delivery strategies for children and families

(Grisham-Brown, 2001). They may provide direct instruction and work directly with children with delays or disabilities, or may provide consultation to general early childhood educators and others who serve them. In all cases, they collaborate with other professionals and families, which calls for such critical communication techniques as listening, questioning, and problem-solving, as well as consultation skills.

Possible Challenges for the Early Childhood Special Educator on the Team and Strategies To Address These Challenges

In recent years, services in EI/ECSE have shifted toward collaboration with other disciplines and services provided in the natural environment, which has presented some unique challenges to the early childhood special educator. Perhaps the most critical questions posed by the early childhood special educator are, "How do I provide service in the natural environment" and "What is my role on the team?" In the past, the early childhood special educator was prepared to directly provide services to young children with special needs. Little emphasis was placed on serving children without disabilities, providing support and consultation to other adults (i.e., professionals from other disciplines, family members), or functioning as a member of a team.

Today, early childhood special educators find themselves filling multiple roles in a variety of positions. For example, the early childhood special educator may be the lead teacher, serving children both with and without special needs in inclusive settings, or may provide home-based services. The early childhood special educator may fill indirect service delivery roles that call for acting as a consultant to and collaborator with general early childhood educators. Early childhood special educators and general early childhood educators often struggle with the definition of their unique roles on the team. Differences in the early childhood educator's and early childhood special educator's roles exist in the manner in which and degree to which they implement each role. For example, the early childhood educator's primary roles in conducting assessment may be in conducting screening or in using informal procedures, such as observation, whereas the early childhood special educator performs those assessment activities and, in addition, conducts diagnostic assessment, employing criterion-referenced measures for instructional programming, and synthesizes results into written reports.

Central to addressing the issue of fulfilling the early childhood special educator's roles and responsibilities in the context of the natural environment is establishing clear roles and responsibilities—both for the early childhood special educator and other members of the team. Once these roles and responsibilities have been created, ample time for planning will be needed and clear pathways of communication must be established. These three components—clear roles and responsibilities, planning, and communication—are central to the early childhood special educator's success in providing services in the natural environment. Over time, the early childhood special educator will become more comfortable in his or her role of providing support within the context of the natural environment and with the general early childhood educator's ability to work with young children with disabilities.

As a member of the team focused on meeting the needs of Javier and his family, the early childhood special educator would have several concerns. Perhaps the greatest concern would be how to provide support to Javier within the context of the kindergarten classroom. The early childhood special educator may feel uncomfortable with the placement of a child with significant needs in an inclusive classroom and may even believe that the general educator does not have the skills necessary to serve the child. It will be important for the early childhood special educator and kindergarten teacher, as well as the other team members, to work collaboratively in addressing some of Javier's most significant challenges (such as temper tantrums, communication issues, and physical needs). The early childhood special educator will need to provide the necessary support to the kindergarten teacher from the beginning so that she is not overwhelmed. Such support will include the establishment of clear roles and responsibilities, mechanisms for planning, team-teaching processes, and ongoing communication. Because of Javier's significant needs, the early childhood special educator and kindergarten teacher must establish a close and effective working relationship.

The family's approach to self-care issues is another major concern of the early childhood special educator. One of the goals of early intervention/education is to foster independence in children. Early childhood special educators would struggle with this issue because it would be important for them to honor the family's desires, but they also would want to do what they believed was in the best interests of the child. Ongoing communication with the family and other team members will be needed to resolve issues associated with Javier's independence.

Summary
Early childhood special education is a profession that is concerned with providing support to young children with known or suspected disabilities and their families. Clearly, the competence and collaborative skills of early childhood special educators is key to providing high-quality EI/ECSE services. If early childhood special educators possess the requisite knowledge and professional skills, coupled with appropriate interpersonal characteristics, attitudes, and behaviors, needed for collaboration, then young children and their families will benefit.

References
Grisham-Brown, J. (2001). Transdisciplinary activity-based assessment for young children with multiple disabilities. *Young Exceptional Children, 3*(2), 3-10.

Individuals With Disabilities Education Improvement Act, 20 U.S.C. §602 (2004).

Kilgo, J., & Bruder, M. B. (1997). Creating new visions in institutions of higher education: Interdisciplinary approaches to personnel preparation in early intervention. In P. J. Winton, J. A. McCollum, & C. Catlett (Eds.), *Reforming personnel preparation in early intervention: Issues, models, and practical strategies* (pp. 81-101). Baltimore: Paul H. Brookes.

Miller, P., & Stayton, V. (2005). Recommended practices in personnel preparation. In S. Sandall, M. L. Hemmeter, B. Smith, & M. McLean (Eds.), *DEC recommended practices: A comprehensive guide for practical application in early intervention/early childhood special education* (pp. 77-88). Longmont, CO: Sopris West.

Sandall, S., Hemmeter, M. L., Smith, B. J., & McLean, M. (Eds.). (2005). *DEC recommended practices: A comprehensive guide for practical application in early intervention/early childhood special education.* Longmont, CO: Sopris West.

Stayton, V., Miller, P., & Dinnebeil, L. (2003). *Personnel preparation in early childhood special education: Implementing the DEC Recommended Practices.* Longmont, CO: Sopris West.

Chapter 5

WHAT OTHERS SHOULD KNOW ABOUT GENERAL EARLY CHILDHOOD EDUCATORS

— Jerry Aldridge

The field of general early childhood education encompasses children from birth through age 8. Children within this age range may attend any one or more of a host of programs serving young children, depending on the region of the world in which they live and their economic circumstances. For example, children from low-income families in the United States may attend an Even Start or Head Start program, a public pre-kindergarten, a foundation- or grant-supported preschool, or other program until they are required by law to begin public school (Morrison, 2004). Some countries, such as Denmark, provide preschool opportunities for most of their children, while other countries, such as Kenya, are just now beginning to provide educational experiences for young children.

Educational Preparation of the General Early Childhood Educator

Both paraprofessionals and professionals work in the field of general early childhood education. Paraprofessionals include child care workers and preschool teachers who have a high school diploma or less. The National Association for the Education of Young Children (NAEYC) and the World Organization for Early Childhood Education (OMEP) both have published guidelines for early childhood education and care. NAEYC implements a Child Development Associate (CDA) program for paraprofessionals. This program is often offered in conjunction with an associate degree at a junior college or four-year institution. Many other agencies also are involved in the delivery of workshops and certificate programs in early childhood education, depending on the country (Hyson, 2003).

Professionals in general early childhood education are required to have a bachelor's degree in early childhood education or a related field. For example, each state in the United States has determined requirements for early childhood professionals. Many general early childhood professionals teach in public school prekindergarten, kindergarten, or early elementary (primary) school programs. The educational requirements and curricula for early childhood education personnel preparation programs are usually grounded in the developmentally appropriate practice guidelines as published by NAEYC (Bredekamp & Copple, 1997).

Early childhood professionals must have an array of competencies in the areas of child development knowledge, curriculum integration, social interaction, guidance support and strategies, and diversity accommodations. While the field of early childhood special education is family-based, the area of general early childhood education traditionally has been more child-centered. Early child-

general education

hood educators have limited knowledge and practice in assessment and modifications for children with special needs, which also poses issues for transdisciplinary teaming.

Roles and Contributions of the General Early Childhood Educator on the Team

The general early childhood educator is responsible for providing educational experiences for all children enrolled in a general education program. Ideally, a child with special needs who attends preschool, kindergarten, or the primary grades will spend the majority of the day in the least restrictive environment, which is often determined to be the general early childhood classroom. The general early childhood teacher has the task of including a child with special needs into the program while making the accommodations and modifications necessary for the child to thrive.

She must know how to implement developmentally appropriate practice, which includes age-appropriate, individually appropriate, and culturally appropriate practice (Bredekamp & Copple, 1997). Her role includes communicating these tenets to the transdisciplinary team and explicitly providing information about how instruction is determined and delivered in the general early childhood classroom setting. The general early childhood teacher also must abandon certain traditional notions about early childhood—for example, the idea that the early childhood teacher is the only one in charge of the preschool, kindergarten, or primary classroom. The early childhood teacher must be particularly open to collaboration in order for inclusive services to occur in natural classroom situations and activities. This means sharing the responsibility for the child with other professionals who will work with her in the classroom. The early childhood teacher's role is to be an honest member of the team, expressing her concerns and vulnerabilities related to working with children with special needs in her classroom.

Possible Challenges for the General Early Childhood Educator on the Team and Strategies To Address These Challenges

Incorporating the early childhood educator into a transdisciplinary team approach can present many challenges, most of which center on three main issues: 1) territory, 2) insecurity, and 3) time. The general early childhood education teacher may not want other professionals coming into her classroom, could experience insecurity with regard to competence with children with special needs, and often experiences the frustration of having a limited amount of time to devote to transdisciplinary issues.

As mentioned previously, the general early childhood teacher must give up the belief that this is *her* classroom, and hers alone. Failure to do so will create one of the biggest obstacles for transdisciplinary teaming. It is better to move beyond thinking "This is my classroom and I am in charge" to "I am a team member who will do my best to collaborate for the best possible accommodations and modifications for any child in the program."

Another challenge has to do with a general educator's insecurities. A general early childhood educator, more often than not, has limited training in the education of children with special needs. She may have taken only an introductory course in special education and may believe she does not have sufficient knowledge about disabilities and inclusion. This attitude is more often an obstacle to the team than the general educator's actual lack of knowledge.

Finally, as is true for other team members, time constrains can pose a real problem. Most general educators do not have the luxury of an extended planning time during the day. Classroom schedules are often inflexible and there may not be someone available to work with the class while the general educator attends transdisciplinary meetings. Frustration over this perceived lack of time often spills over into a belief that "I already have too much to do and now I am expected to work harder to work with a child and a team that I do not understand."

The importance of administrative support cannot be overstated, as an appropriate amount of time needs to be set aside for effective teaming to occur.

To address these obstacles or challenges, the early childhood teacher must be welcomed as a vital member of the team. The team will collaborate more effectively if the other members acknowledge that while many of the accommodations and modifications will occur in the general classroom, they are there to provide support and make the task easier. While the attitude "This is *my* classroom" is difficult to change, the acceptance of the general educator as a vital, equal member of the team will help resolve that issue.

In another strategy, other team members provide the general education teacher with information about the child's disability and specific needs as the transdisciplinary team begins to work together. This approach should be handled in a positive, nonthreatening way. For example, the early childhood special educator might say, "I know how busy you are and I happened to find this article or this information that was helpful to me concerning the child's disability. I thought you might like a copy." Providing information will go a long way in easing the general educator's feelings of uncertainty about best addressing the child's needs.

The lack of time is often the most difficult obstacle to overcome—all team members face this challenge. However, the general early childhood educator often believes that she is the only one making a time sacrifice. After all, she is with the children most of the day. This attitude may result in the teacher setting up a somewhat inflexible schedule during the hours when children are in her program. Whenever possible, team meetings should not interrupt the classroom day. If necessary to do so, other team members can acknowledge the difficulties of meeting during class time and plan for other meetings that do not interrupt the teacher's time with children during the school day. Administrative support is needed in establishing the timetable for team meetings.

A child like Javier presents numerous challenges for the general educator. At least six interrelated issues may confront the early childhood educator: 1) fear of dealing with a disability such as spina bifida, 2) anxiety about physical injury, 3) worries about emergency procedures, 4) concerns about social interaction, 5) concerns about cultural issues, and 6) problems with language barriers.

The general early childhood teacher may have a fear of working with any child with a disability such as spina bifida. Because children with neural tube differences pose special challenges, the general education teacher could be overly frightened about the fragile nature of a child with spina bifida. The nurse practitioner, occupational therapist, physical therapist, and early childhood special educator are presented with the additional challenge of helping the general educator work through these fears.

One reason the general educator may fear working with Javier is a fear of him being physically injured. A good early childhood educator provides for active learning activities that involve a lot of movement throughout the day. Other children, especially if they are highly active, also may provide challenges. It may or may not be a legitimate fear, but the general education teacher may be concerned that another child will kick or hit Javier, creating a life-threatening medical emergency. As a result, the teacher may become overprotective and restrict children's active movement or social interactions.

The general early childhood educator may obsess over emergency procedures and how to competently handle Javier in a medical situation. Again, the nurse, occupational therapist, physical therapist, and early childhood special educator can assist by acknowledging the teacher's fears and providing the information and support for the teacher to be confident she can handle the situation if such an episode occurs.

All of these concerns can inhibit the teacher's desire to provide natural, appropriate social interactions between Javier and his peers. Javier could become isolated in his wheelchair or other supportive devices if the teacher is concerned that other children could harm Javier. These fears may be unfounded, but they are real to the general education teacher. Other team members can help by being supportive and providing as much specific information as possible as it relates to the handling or positioning of Javier for optimal social interaction.

Cultural issues also are a concern for the general education teacher. In the United States, a general early childhood teacher grounded in developmentally appropriate practice often seeks to promote autonomy and independence in her children. By contrast, many parents from Mexico (and possibly other countries) often believe that achieving autonomy and independence should be postponed until their children are older. Javier's disability compounds this issue as his parents' goals for him do not include autonomy and independence. The issue of the parents' immigration status also may be a concern for Javier's teacher. She may be hesitant to provide information because she is uncertain about the rights and services available to individuals who are undocumented. Simply put, she doesn't want to get Javier's parents in trouble while they seek appropriate services for him. In addition, the general early childhood educator does not speak Spanish, and Javier's mother does not speak English, which exacerbates the cultural barriers between Javier's family and the teacher.

The general early childhood education teacher needs extra support and encouragement from the other transdisciplinary team members with regard to Javier. Because the teacher has many concerns about being able to meet the needs of a child with spina bifida, other team members may need to take the lead in recommending appropriate accommodations and modifications, as well as providing the assistance necessary for the teacher to feel comfortable. All team members must convey to the parents that they are "on the same page" in their recommendations for Javier's education and support.

Summary

General early childhood education as a profession is concerned with supporting the learning and overall development of young children. The profession has a long history of teaching young children in a variety of education settings, including preschool, kindergarten, and early primary settings. The most challenging obstacles for early childhood educators who serve as members of transdisciplinary teams include meeting the needs of *all* children in the classroom and coordinating with the other team members in order to do so.

References

Bredekamp, S., & Copple, C. (Eds.). (1997). *Developmentally appropriate practice in early childhood programs* (Rev. ed.). Washington, DC: National Association for the Education of Young Children.

Hyson, M. (Ed.). (2003). *Preparing early childhood professionals: NAEYC's standards for programs-NAEYC's standards for initial licensure, advanced, and associate degree programs.* Washington, DC: National Association for the Education of Young Children.

Morrison, G. (2004). *Early childhood education today* (10th ed.). Columbus, OH: Pearson: Merrill/Prentice-Hall.

Chapter 6

WHAT OTHERS SHOULD KNOW ABOUT COMMUNICATION DISORDER PROFESSIONALS: SPEECH~LANGUAGE PATHOLOGY AND AUDIOLOGY

Cathy Burke

Speech-language pathologists and audiologists assess and provide intervention for people with communication disorders. Speech-language pathologists (SLPs) work with children and/or adults who have difficulties in such areas as comprehending speech, expressing themselves, speaking clearly, etc. Speech-language pathologists are sometimes referred to as SLPs, speech pathologists, speech therapists, or communication specialists. Audiologists identify hearing loss through various assessment procedures, prescribe and fit hearing aids and other forms of assistive listening devices, and may provide some intervention. Speech-language pathologists and audiologists work in a variety of settings, including community agencies, early intervention programs, school systems, hospitals, clinics, and private practices (Hamaguchi, 1995).

Educational Preparation

In order to practice independently, a speech-language pathologist should have a master's degree in speech-language pathology and be certified through the American Speech-Language-Hearing Association (ASHA). The certification is called the Certificate of Clinical Competence (CCC). Most states also require the SLP to have a license. An SLP working in a school system also may be required to have some type of teaching credential.

An SLP who has a bachelor's degree in speech-language pathology may be able to practice as a speech-language pathology aide. She or he can provide therapy under the supervision of a certified SLP, but cannot conduct evaluations or develop intervention goals or programs (these should be done by the certified SLP).

An audiologist currently must have a master's degree in audiology and be certified through ASHA. By 2007, however, the entry level for independent practice will be a doctoral degree in audiology (the AuD). The requirement for a doctoral degree is mandatory for persons who apply for certification after December 31, 2011. Most states require an audiologist to have state licensure as well.

The American Speech-Language-Hearing Association (ASHA) is the professional, scientific, and credentialing association for audiologists, speech-language pathologists, and speech, language, and hearing scientists. ASHA's mission is to promote the interests of, and provide the highest quality services for, professionals in audiology, speech-language pathology, and speech and hearing science, and to advocate for people with communication disabilities (see ASHA's Web site). The ASHA Code of Ethics states that SLPs and audiologists should work only within their "Scope of Practice," which means that one should practice only in areas in which one is competent, based on education, training, and experience (ASHA, 1999).

Roles and Contributions of the Speech-Language Pathologist on the Team

The roles and responsibilities of a speech-language pathologist who works with young children have expanded in the past few years. Assessment-related roles not only include screenings (to identify children with possible communication difficulties) and formal and informal evaluations (to determine if a communication delay or disorder is present in the areas of speech, receptive language, expressive language, oral motor abilities, prelinguistic communication, social communication, and assistive technology), but now place an even greater emphasis on the following:

- Interpreting communication assessment results to family and other team members; relating findings to other areas of the child's development when appropriate (e.g., hearing, cognition, behavior, motor skills, etc)
- Helping to identify child's strengths and needs and their impact on participation in daily routines at home and school
- Educating family and other team members about communication delays and disorders, and their impact on a child's development, learning, and everyday life
- Educating family members, educational staff, related service providers, and other team members about typical communication development, including the areas of: 1) speech, oral motor, and feeding; 2) prelinguistic and early developing cognitive skills; and 3) auditory skills, receptive language, expressive language, and social communication abilities.

With regard to intervention, the SLP's therapy roles traditionally have been viewed as providing direct therapy and indirect consultation. According to McCormick, Loeb, and Schiefelbush (1997), these roles have expanded to include (among other areas):

- Helping the family and other team members: 1) develop goals and objectives; 2) identify needed information, materials, and/or equipment; 3) select the most appropriate intervention strategies and techniques; 4) plan activities; 5) provide support to other team members responsible for carrying out plans; and 6) determine location(s), type, and frequency of communication services
- Designing and implementing a range of intervention programs
- Helping family and other team members learn to use important strategies and techniques to encourage the child's communication skills at home and in child care settings, school, and other community settings
- Collaborating with others to encourage the child's active participation in age-appropriate activities with typically developing, same-age peers in a variety of natural settings
- Providing a greater range of speech-language intervention services (e.g., direct therapy, consultation, collaborative intervention, co-teaching with early childhood teacher and/or early childhood special education teacher)
- Participating in ongoing problem solving and decision-making with other team members regarding assessment and monitoring of program effectiveness.

When serving children who demonstrate language impairments in a primary language that is not English, ASHA stresses the importance of strong collaboration between the SLP and the ESL professional, particularly on the following issues and areas:

- Exchanging information on various language issues, such as language development, code switching, development of language proficiency, patterns of first and second language development, and language use in the classroom versus home

- Sharing and interpreting assessment results
- Developing an appropriate intervention plan, which should include: 1) adapting curricula to meet the child's specific needs, such as modifying assignments, activities, and tests; 2) considering the individual child's needs and learning style; 3) selecting appropriate materials and instructional strategies; and 4) involving caregivers in the child's program of instruction
- Collaborating with family and other educational staff on a regular basis; their intervention roles may include: 1) sharing ideas and resources as well as planning and working together to coordinate goals and objectives, 2) monitoring progress toward speech and/or language intervention goals and English language development goals, 3) coordinating the instruction of English language development with the intervention for the communication disorder
- Considering cultural and linguistic factors that affect service delivery
- Preparing and participating in IFSP/IEP reviews.

In the absence of an ESL program, an administrator may ask an SLP to provide ESL services (particularly in geographical areas with limited resources), although most SLPs have not been trained to provide ESL services. ASHA has directed SLPs to provide ESL services only if they have acquired the necessary knowledge and skill level through specialized training and experience (ASHA, 1997). ASHA (1997) directs the SLP who has not been trained in ESL to serve as a consultant to the child's primary caregivers, classroom teacher, and other professionals, and to advocate for the child to professionals and other agencies.

Roles and Contributions of the Audiologist on the Team

Audiologists who work with young children provide a range of services (ASHA, 2002). Roles and responsibilities may include the following:

- Providing hearing conservation programs to help prevent hearing loss or minimize its impact
- Conducting a variety of hearing screenings (universal newborn screenings through otoacoustic emission [OAE], individual audiological screenings, group audiological screenings) to rule out hearing loss; screens for ear disorders and related disabilities; uses at-risk criteria for infants and toddlers
- Evaluating hearing loss, using a range of procedures, including otoacoustic emission (OAE), audiological pure tone testing (whereby the child raises his hand or drops a toy in a container when he hears certain sounds or tones), and brainstem auditory evoked response (BAER)
- Assessing middle ear functioning through tympanometry
- Determining the range, nature, and degree of hearing loss
- Referring to appropriate specialists (speech-language pathologists; pediatricians; ear, nose, and throat specialists; developmental specialists; geneticists; etc.)
- Providing intervention, or habilitative, services, including auditory training, speech reading (lip reading), language habilitation, hearing evaluations, and speech conservation
- Providing counseling to and guidance for children, parents, and teachers regarding hearing loss
- Determining a child's need for group and individual amplification, selecting and fitting an appropriate aid, and evaluating the effectiveness of an aid (examples of hearing-related assistive technology devices including hearing aids, auditory trainers, FM systems, etc.).

Concerns About Javier From the Communication Specialist's Perspective

Family members have not expressed a significant concern about Javier's hearing loss or his delayed communication skills, and they do not seem to have made any changes in the ways they communicate with him at home and in the community. Javier's family and neighbors predominantly speak Spanish to him. Family members often interpret what he is saying (in Spanish and in English) for others; they also explain to him what others are saying. Although they took Javier to his scheduled audiology appointments and received initial education in the care and management of his hearing aids, he often comes to school with nonfunctioning aids (because of dead batteries or missing batteries) or without the hearing aids altogether. School staff, particularly SLPs and educators, often feel frustrated over these types of issues. They believe that Javier could make better progress in communication and academics if he could hear better and if his family would speak English to him. They believe that exposure to one language is critical in order for him to develop competency in oral and written language for social, academic, and future employment reasons (particularly given his cognitive challenges, hearing loss, and other disabilities). And they certainly believe that his progress and development are at greater risk if his hearing is compromised.

If the family could better see how communication plays a role in other aspects of Javier's life that they are greatly concerned about (such as their fears of him being teased by other children) they might, with time, be more motivated to address communication development. The SLP could explain how improving Javier's social language skills may help him learn to make friends and use communication to defend himself as well. The SLP and the audiologist also will need to find ways to remind the family repeatedly about the relationship of hearing and language, again with the hope that appreciating the social aspect of communication might prompt them to make changes in the way they manage and encourage use of his hearing aids. Since the family plans on attending school with Javier on some days, the SLP, audiologist, and ESL teacher can work together to slowly help the Gonzales family recognize how improved communication can empower Javier and help him make and keep friends. Even so, the family still may be more inclined to incorporate some strategies only in Spanish rather than in English. It will be important for all team members to recognize this as an important step, and to continue to seek advice and input from the ESL teacher and other team members knowledgeable about these language and cultural issues.

References

American Speech-Language-Hearing Association. (1997). *Provision of instruction in English as a second language by speech-language pathologists.* Rockville, MD: Author.

American Speech-Language-Hearing Association. (1999). *Code of ethics.* Rockville, MD: Author.

American Speech-Language-Hearing Association. (2002). *Guidelines for audiology service provision in the schools.* Rockville, MD: Author.

Hamaguchi, P. (1995). *Speech, language, and listening problems: What every parent should know.* New York: Wiley and Sons.

McCormick, L., Loeb, D. F., & Schiefelbush, R. L. (1997). *Supporting children with communication difficulties in inclusive settings: School-based language intervention.* Needham Heights, MA: Allyn and Bacon.

Chapter 7

WHAT OTHERS SHOULD KNOW
ABOUT OCCUPATIONAL THERAPISTS

————————————————————————Laura Vogtle

Occupational therapists are professionals who work with individuals to accomplish *purposeful activities* (American Occupational Therapy Association, 2002); that is, activities that are aimed at a personal goal, such as the various tasks that individuals usually perform in a day. For a child, purposeful activities might include getting ready for school (e.g., bathing, dressing, grooming, using the toilet, eating); going to school (e.g., sitting in a car seat, riding the school bus); and doing the things they do at school (e.g., playing with peers, communicating with others, reading). These purposeful activities make up what are called *occupations* (e.g., activities of daily living, school, work, other productive activities, leisure)—those goals or tasks that are personally important and that the person chooses to do (Hinojosa & Blount, 2004). When an occupational therapist provides services, the end goal of that intervention is to help the child/student/client carry out activities that are meaningful and have a definite purpose in his or her life.

Purposeful activities and occupations, as described above, vary considerably across different contextual features such as age, culture, disability, and socioeconomic status. Occupational therapy services are designed to help individuals so that they will be able to carry out or *participate* in the occupations and purposeful activities that are important to them and their family. This is a challenging task that requires the consideration of many factors, including: 1) the physical aspects of the child (his or her strength, coordination, visual skills, and so forth); 2) the desired occupations (participation in school, activities of daily living, work, leisure); 3) the different activities that make up the occupation (for dressing, this would include choosing clothes, getting them from the bureau, putting them on, buttoning and zipping, then carrying out final adjustments); 4) the location of where the occupation will be carried out (home, school); 5) the kinds of existing supports that are available to help the child (assistive technology, environmental modifications, a personal care assistant, modified buses); and 6) the relevant contextual features, such as culture, religion, family preferences, and so forth (Kellegrew & Krosmark, 1999).

Rarely is a professional from one discipline able to meet all of the needs of an individual in a community, school, or health care setting. Occupational therapists must be able to work within a team structure. They need to be able to plan, organize, and execute service plans with other team members, which include the family, teachers, physical therapists, speech-language pathologists, and others. They also need to be able to work in a variety of settings—home, school, playground, child care settings—where children and families participate in activities that are important to them.

Educational Preparation

By 2007, the minimum educational requirements for an occupational therapist will be a master's degree. Students studying to become occupational therapists will get a bachelor's degree in a related field (e.g., biology, psychology, special education), apply to an accredited graduate program in occupational therapy, and proceed to finish what is usually a 7-semester master's degree program. A clinical doctorate (OTD) is available in some programs, which is a longer program of study for a degree that is also used in clinical settings. Regardless of the degree level, all persons in the United States completing an occupational therapy degree who want to be licensed and practice must pass the National Board of Occupational Therapy Certification exam. Forty-six of the 50 states and the District of Columbia require licensure of occupational therapists following passage of the registration exam, with the other 4 states having either certification or another form of regulation. The American Occupational Therapy Association is the national organization that sets standards of practice and professional competency, and regulates and accredits educational institutions.

Roles and Contributions of the Occupational Therapist on the Team

In the United States, the Individuals With Disabilities Education Improvement Act (IDEA) (2004) identifies related service personnel as those who provide transportation and such developmental, corrective, and other supportive services as are required to help a child with a disability benefit from special education (IDEA, 2004). Occupational therapy is designated as a related service under this definition. Related service personnel are part of teams, which include parents, that work with young children who have special needs. Such teams operate within early intervention (Part C) and school system (Part B) guidelines and function as interdisciplinary or transdisciplinary teams. Evaluation procedures are carried out either by individual professionals or by groups of professionals; recommenda-

---

Examples of Occupations and Purposeful Activities of Childhood

Occupation	Purposeful Activities
Play	Reach, grasp, manipulate, and release objects
	Visual, auditory, and tactile exploration of toys
	Remove from/replace toys to appropriate storage location
	Organize/sequence activities for desired outcomes
	Play with others
Activities of Daily Living	Eating (pick up utensils; scoop food; chew and swallow; pick up, drink from, and put down cup)
	Dressing (don and doff clothing, do fasteners)
	Toileting (don and doff clothing, use toilet)
	Hygiene (wiping face after meals, washing hands)
Written Communication	Color (hold crayons, support paper, make appropriate lines and shapes)
	Use scissors (hold scissors, support paper, snip and cut on lines)
	Print (hold writing utensil, support paper, produce symbols in a legible manner)
	Write (hold writing utensil, support paper, produce symbols in a legible manner)
	Use the computer (turn on computer, access program, use keyboard, save files, close out programs, print)

Figure 7.1

tions for service provision are developed from the results of those evaluations and from recommendations of the team according to individual state guidelines.

In the framework of early intervention and school systems, occupational therapists provide interventions aimed at helping young children and their families carry out the kinds of occupations that children who are typically developing do. This means that occupational therapists assist in the development of the skills needed for children to be able to do purposeful activities and occupations, such as those described in Figure 1.

Just like teachers and other related service personnel, occupational therapists help to develop goals/outcomes for the individualized family service plan (IFSP) or individualized education program (IEP) in the legally mandated format if the child qualifies for services. The frequency and duration of services is listed in the IFSP/IEP. Ideally, all team members agree on the goals/outcomes for individual children and work together to support these goals/outcomes (Barnes & Turner, 2001).

In order to address the needs of young children with special needs, occupational therapists use many tools. They may incorporate direct intervention, modifications to the environment, assistive technology, peer supports, and requests for the rest of the team to promote certain behaviors. To achieve effective change, such methods should produce outcomes that can be documented (King et al., 1999).

Possible Challenges of the Occupational Therapist on the Team and Strategies To Address These Challenges

Service provision and all the ramifications of service provision usually work well when the occupational therapist is hired to work full-time by the school system or agency, rather than on an hourly contractual basis. However, many school systems or agencies cannot afford to have a full-time staff of therapists, and so hire occupational therapy services on a contractual basis. This means that the occupational therapist has to achieve all of his or her work within the contract limits. For example, an occupational therapist may be hired to work 8 hours a week to provide services to a caseload of 10 children, document the treatment, communicate with teachers and other team members, and be present for meetings. Because occupational, as well as physical, therapists bill for their services in subcontract situations, the time they spend on the job is monitored carefully by company management, limiting their flexibility in those settings where they practice. Occupational therapists working for a school system often have their own challenges. They are usually responsible for a number of schools, which requires regular travel. Additionally, space for evaluation and treatment is often at a premium within schools. Time for meetings and communication with other team members frequently is limited.

While such challenges seem formidable, creative team members can work around them with patience, flexibility, and cooperation. The use of logs, E-mail, and telephone conferences can facilitate communication. Creating a format for specific documentation of concerns for individual children can help a busy therapist understand a problem clearly. Incorporating therapy within the classroom for purposeful activities, such as computer access, writing, and some self-care activities, can alleviate space issues and allow teachers and other team members to see recommendations in action. Studies have indicated that incorporating the context of the classroom into service provision (Kellegrew, 1996) has its advantages. In spite of the special challenges that face occupational therapists in the school system, work in school environments remains one of the primary employment options for occupational therapists. Over time, most therapists working in schools are very positive about the team-based approach to addressing the needs of children with disabilities and their families.

Aspects of occupational therapy intervention will be discussed in the sections that follow, based on the case study of Javier described in Chapter 3. The occupational therapy services are discussed in relation to early intervention, Head Start, and transition to kindergarten.

Early Intervention Services. Until Javier reached the age of 3, services were delivered in his home. The agency providing services used a transdisciplinary model of intervention, meaning that one team member provided the actual services, with input and instruction from other team members. The first primary service provider for Javier was a physical therapist; later, the educator took over that role. The occupational therapist focused on developing occupations for Javier that were age appropriate, but his limited hand function skills—difficulties with grasp, coordination, and strength—proved to be an obstacle. Children with spina bifida often use their upper limbs for support and mobility, limiting the time they have for play that involves hand function; they also often have neurological problems that can affect their hand use.

The occupational therapist also was concerned that Javier become more adept at such purposeful activities as finger feeding and holding a bottle. However, Javier's family, from their cultural perspective, did not consider the goals of independence to be important. This was a difficult issue for the occupational therapist, as well as the rest of the team, who struggled with the cultural differences regarding performance issues. This struggle underscored the need for team members to be aware of differences associated with culture and the perspective of undocumented immigrants regarding legal issues, gender interaction differences, the role of extended family, perspectives on disabilities, approaches to timeliness, the perceived status of health care professionals, verbal and emotional expression, religious beliefs and practices, and language barriers (Moxley, Mahendra, & Vega-Barachowitz, 2004).

The professionals on the team had many difficult conversations regarding the Gonzales family's goals for Javier. As strong as the team members' opinions were on such issues as managing Javier's tantrums, the family's approach to self-care, and the team members' frustration with the Gonzaleses' tardiness, their planned pilgrimage, and the continuing telephone calls, they knew they had to broach these issues carefully. The physical therapist and the educator periodically would demonstrate teaching certain behaviors to Javier, but the family's preferences in these areas served as the guideline by which the team worked.

The occupational therapist met with the team on a regular basis to listen to feedback regarding Javier's progress. Suggestions and reminders relating to the areas of concern were folded into the primary intervention provider's repertoire as necessary. The occupational therapist accompanied the primary service provider on home visits once every 3-4 months, in order to observe changes and update information as needed.

Head Start Services. As noted in Chapter 3, Javier began attending Head Start at age 3. At this point, he was in a center-based, rather than a home-based, program. The concerns regarding Javier's occupational therapy within the Head Start program focused on his delays in dressing skills and his fine and visual motor skills, such as object assembly (e.g., using Legos or blocks), crayon use, and sequencing activities. Occupational therapy services were delivered on a monthly consultant basis. Javier's family was protective and continued to do things for him that he was capable of performing himself; this problem was more apparent than when he was receiving early intervention services, as he was older and more was expected of him. The team believed that Javier's tantrums had increased due to the family's cosseting and their need to prevent his crying. Nevertheless, it was necessary to listen carefully to the family's concerns and negotiate the intervention emphasis toward those aspects of Javier's performance most critical to his future functioning at school, while still hearing what was most important to the family at home. The team included the family as a team member, but it was a continuous challenge to listen to what the family had to say rather than pushing the professionals' intervention agenda. Team members engaged in continuous open discussions regarding cultural issues, clarifying professional and family frustrations and enabling all team members to have a sense of humor regarding those aspects of Javier's care that provoked disagreement.

Transition to Kindergarten. When it came time for Javier to enter kindergarten, the Head Start personnel, kindergarten teachers, Javier's father, and the related services personnel all met to plan for the coming change. Initially, the most pressing concern centered on deciding which school was the most appropriate. Once this decision was made, the team began to develop those overarching goals for Javier that they saw as critical to his successful inclusion into the school. The team acknowledged that considerable work remained related to how the family approached Javier's tantrums and self-care activities, as well as with the family's trust in, and interactions with, the system.

The occupational therapist's specific concerns for Javier continued to be in the areas of tantrum management, dressing, and hand function. His dressing needs were expanded to cover some aspects of lower extremity dressing (related to his toileting needs). The school nurse would conduct Javier's catheterization and, in conjunction with her discussion with the occupational therapist, would encourage Javier to unfasten and pull down his pants so she can do this.

Javier's delays in propelling his wheelchair have caused other children in the Head Start class to take care of him rather than facilitating him to do more on his own. The peers saw him as needing help rather than being able to care for himself and contribute to the class. These kinds of issues need to be considered and addressed by the whole team in the neighborhood school. The team agreed it was important to be consistent in their message to peers regarding how to manage Javier's classroom skills.

References

American Occupational Therapy Association. (2002). Occupational therapy practice framework: Domain and process. *American Journal of Occupational Therapy, 56*, 609-639.

Barnes, K. J., & Turner, K. D. (2001). Team collaborative practices between teachers and occupational therapists. *American Journal of Occupational Therapy, 55*, 83-89.

Hinojosa, J., & Blount, M. L. (2004). Purposeful activities within the context of occupational therapy. In J. Hinojosa & M. L. Blount (Eds.), *The texture of life* (2nd ed., pp 1-16). Bethesda, MD: American Occupational Therapy Association.

Individuals With Disabilities Education Improvement Act, 20 U.S.C. §602 (2004).

Kellegrew, D. (1996, Oct.). Occupational therapy in full-inclusion classrooms: A case study from the Moorpark model. *American Journal of Occupational Therapy, 50*(9), 718-724.

Kellegrew, D., & Krosmark, U. (1999). Examining school routines using time-geography methodology. *Physical and Occupational Therapy in Pediatrics, 19*(2), 79-91.

King, G., McDougall, J., Tucker, M. A., Gritzan, J., Malloy-Miller, T., Alambets, P., Cunning, D., Thomas, K., & Gregory, K. (1999). An evaluation of functional, school-based therapy services for children with special needs. *Physical and Occupational Therapy in Pediatrics, 19*(2), 5-29.

Moxley, A., Mahendra, N., & Vega-Barachowitz, C. (2004). Cultural competence in health care. *The ASHA Leader,* 6-21.

Chapter 8

What Others Should Know
About Physical Therapists

—Betty Denton & Rachael Rose

Physical therapy is a health care profession focused on the diagnosis and management of movement dysfunctions and the enhancement of physical and functional activities for persons across the entire age range. Physical therapists work directly with individuals, utilizing a variety of hands-on means to restore, maintain, and promote optimal physical function as it relates to movement and health, as well as optimal wellness, fitness, and quality of life. Physical therapy is also concerned with preventing the onset, symptoms, and progression of impairments, functional limitations, and disabilities that may result from diseases, disorders, conditions, or injuries (American Physical Therapy Association, 2001a). Physical therapy is provided in a variety of settings to individuals with a wide range of problems that are present at birth or shortly after, that are due to injury, or that are a result of the aging process. The American Physical Therapy Association (APTA) is the largest national professional organization representing the profession of physical therapy. Its goal is to foster advancements in physical therapy practice, research, and education.

Physical therapists have provided services to children with special needs ever since the profession began in the early 1920s. Services used to be primarily provided within health care settings. With the passage of the Education of all Handicapped Children Act (PL94-142) in the mid 1970s, physical therapy services began to be offered within the school setting. The act designated physical therapy as a "related service," which was defined as a supportive service to help children benefit from special education. The Individuals With Disabilities Education Act (IDEA) extended services to infants and toddlers with disabilities; consequently, physical therapy was designated as an early intervention service. Within this expanded role for physical therapy, physical therapists work directly with young children and collaboratively with educators, family members, and other professionals to meet the special learning and developmental needs of the children.

Educational Preparation of Physical Therapists

Physical therapy services are provided by licensed physical therapists, who may deliver the services directly or delegate specific elements of the service, once the therapist has determined the physical therapy plan of care, to a physical therapist assistant or other support personnel who are trained and supervised by the physical therapist. Physical therapists must be licensed to practice by a licensing board within each state where the therapist practices. In order to be licensed, the physical therapist must be a graduate of an accredited educational program and must pass a national licensing examination. The legal parameters determining the practice of physical therapy are somewhat variable from state to state. (For example, in some states it would be legal for a physical therapist to examine and provide intervention to a child at the request of a parent, while in another state a referral from a physician would be legally required before a physical therapist could serve a child in any setting.)

physical therapists

Currently, there are 204 educational programs for physical therapists located within institutions of higher learning in the United States. The Commission on Accreditation in Physical Therapy Education (CAPTE) of the American Physical Therapy Association (APTA) sets the standards for education and is the accrediting body for all educational programs. All programs at the graduate level require 2.5 to 4 years (depending upon the specific institutional requirements) of professional education following completion of a baccalaureate degree. The requirements for completing a baccalaureate degree vary, but applicants to physical therapy education programs must meet certain prerequisite coursework requirements, which include the physical, biological, and psychosocial sciences. All education programs providing entry-level physical therapy education award either a master's degree or a doctoral degree. All of the professional education programs include both academic (didactic) instructional components and clinical instructional components. Graduates of physical therapy educational programs are prepared to meet the needs of a diverse population of individuals of all ages, including children with known or suspected disabilities. Once physical therapy students have successfully completed the education requirements, they are eligible to sit for a national licensure exam.

Licensed, practicing physical therapists may specialize in certain areas of practice, such as pediatrics, following their entry-level education. This specialization may emerge as an individual therapist chooses to focus his or her practice on a particular population. Therapists may become board-certified clinical specialists in certain areas of practice, one of which is pediatrics. If they elect to become a certified clinical specialist, they must meet practice and knowledge requirements, as well as pass a certification examination administered by the American Board of Physical Therapy Specialties. Currently, there are 524 pediatric clinical specialists (PCS) across the United States. Clinical specialist certification is a voluntary process and not a requirement for employment. In addition, physical therapists can be certified in specific treatment techniques, such as neurodevelopmental treatment (NDT).

The majority of physical therapists are found in various health care settings, ranging from hospitals to outpatient clinics, skilled nursing facilities, and homes; however, roughly 5 percent of physical therapists practice in such settings as schools or agencies serving the needs of infants and children with special needs (APTA, 2001b). In these types of settings, physical therapists may be employees of the facility or agency, or they may be self-employed and have a contract arrangement to provide physical therapy services to the facility or agency. Often, the physical therapist may be providing services to multiple programs and sites at the same time.

Possible Challenges Facing the Physical Therapist on the Team and Strategies To Address These Challenges

As a member of the team focusing on meeting the needs of Javier and his family, the physical therapist will be especially interested in Javier's ability to move and function in the environment at home, school, and the community. While Javier's family currently prefers to carry him when at home and in the community, as Javier grows older and larger, this method of mobility will become less socially acceptable as well as more physically difficult for his family. There are also concerns about damage to his skin as he pulls himself around on the floor at home. In the school setting at Head Start, Javier has utilized the wheelchair for mobility, but is somewhat limited in his abilities. Because Javier will be at school for longer periods of time, positioning during the day will be important. Javier will need to begin using the dynamic stander and his braces as a part of his daily routine. The neighborhood school personnel are likely to need assistance in learning about appropriate application of the various pieces of equipment, the safest and most optimal transfer techniques, and setting appropriate expectations for Javier's independent and/or assisted use of the wheelchair in the school and on the bus.

The physical therapist will need to spend time with the kindergarten teachers, special education resource teacher, physical education teacher, bus driver, and aides at the neighborhood school to provide them with instruction in wheelchair maneuvering, safety, and transfers. The physical therapist also must be open to meeting the needs of the school personnel, recognizing that each person's knowledge of interacting with a child with spina bifida may differ. In addition, the therapist should explore with the teacher the need for providing information about spina bifida to the other children in Javier's kindergarten class. For example, the physical therapist can help arrange for members of "Kids on the Block," an educational puppet show that is widely used throughout the United States, to come to the school and perform a program focused on a child with spina bifida. In addition to performing the puppet show, "Kids on the Block" provides the children and teachers with a booklet about spina bifida called "Just Like You" (Children's Health System, 2003). The physical therapist can offer to participate during the discussion when this booklet is read in the classroom.

The physical therapist should develop and maintain communication with the physical therapist who provides services at the state rehabilitation agency's spina bifida clinic, so that any of Javier's particular medical or equipment issues can be incorporated into the planning for his kindergarten experience. In addition, the therapists from the two agencies should communicate regarding family education and home program recommendations, so as to avoid giving conflicting messages to the family. Ultimately, during IEP meetings or during informal communications with the family, the physical therapist must convey that all who are involved with Javier's management are "on the same page."

References

American Physical Therapy Association. (2001a). *Guide to physical therapist practice* (2nd ed.). Alexandria, VA: Author.
American Physical Therapy Association. (2001b). *Employment survey*. Alexandria, VA: Author.
Children's Health System. (2003). *Just like you (A booklet about spina bifida for K-2nd grade)*. Birmingham, AL: CHECK Center, Children's Hospital of Alabama.

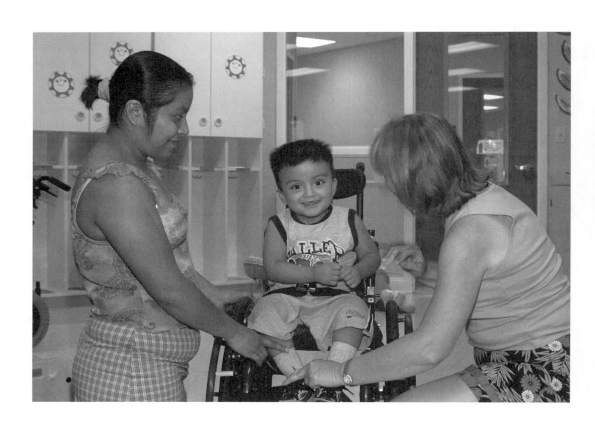

Chapter 9

WHAT OTHERS SHOULD KNOW
ABOUT PROFESSIONAL NURSES

——————————————————————*Janice Vincent & Margie Findley*

Throughout its history, the nursing profession has sought to define its specific roles and responsibilities. The International Council of Nurses (ICN) defines nursing as a profession that encompasses autonomous and collaborative care of individuals of all ages, families, groups and communities, sick or well, and in all settings. Nursing includes the promotion of health, prevention of illness, and the care of ill, disabled, and dying people. Advocacy, promotion of a safe environment, research, participation in shaping health policy and in patient and health systems management, and education are also key nursing roles (ICN, 2004).

Ultimately, the definition of the nursing practice is the responsibility of each state. The Board of Nursing for each state provides the legal definition of nursing as practiced within the state's boundaries, and delineates the nurse's scope of practice. The state's Board of Nursing licenses the professional nurse after he or she successfully passes a national licensure exam following graduation from a basic education program. Nationally recognized professional nursing roles include: caregiver, educator, client advocate, counselor, leader/manager, collaborator, change agent, and researcher.

The professional nurse can work in a variety of settings, such as hospitals, clinics, schools, community centers, higher education facilities, health departments, research facilities, and government agencies. Regardless of the setting, the nurse is concerned with the well-being of the client within the context of the family, the client's health status, and the environment in which the client interacts. In other words, the nurse uses a holistic approach to the client, viewing the client as a whole person interacting within an environment. This holistic approach enables the nurse to best help individuals and their families "maintain autonomy in making decisions that promote wellness across the life span" (Morse, 1994, p. 41).

Educational Preparation of the Professional Nurse

An individual must progress through three basic levels before taking the national licensure exam for a professional nurse: diploma (3 years of basic education, usually in a hospital-based school of nursing), associate degree in nursing (2 years at a community college), and baccalaureate degree in nursing (4 years in a university setting). In addition to the basic levels, professional nurses also can achieve an advanced practice degree. They can receive a master's of science in nursing, with a specialty practice as a clinical nurse specialist, certified registered nurse practitioner, certified nurse midwife, certified registered nurse anesthetist, or higher education educator; and they can pursue a doctoral degree (Ph.D., DSN, DNSc).

The American Nurses Association (ANA) is the primary professional nursing organization in the United States. The ANA ensures nursing quality through maintaining the Code of Ethics for Nurses and develops and publishes the *Scope and Standards of Practice for Nursing*. In addition, the ANA addresses workplace hazards and promotes practices that ensure an optimal work environment for professional nurses. The ANA is active in lobbying on health care issues and health care policy at the federal and state levels (ANA, 2004).

The Developmental Disabilities Nurses Association (DDNA) is a specialty nursing organization that was founded in 1992 to serve the professional needs of nurses who provide care for individuals with developmental disabilities. The mission of DDNA is to continually develop the expertise of the professional nurse in order to improve the lives of individuals with developmental disabilities. Through this organization, professional nurses are able to explore common issues and concerns, obtain continuing education, and receive recognition within their specialty area. The association published the premier issue of the *International Journal of Nursing in Intellectual and Developmental Disabilities* in 2004. This electronic, peer-reviewed journal provides a medium through which international experts can readily and economically share information with professional nurses (www.ddna.org).

The DDNA has established a national professional certification for registered nurses. Becoming certified as a developmental disabilities nurse (CDDN) allows nurses to demonstrate knowledge and skills beyond their basic credentials. Certification demonstrates a commitment to the nursing profession and to the provision of quality care for individuals with developmental disabilities.

Roles and Contributions of the Professional Nurse on the Team

Nurses from a variety of practice areas can be invaluable to the transdisciplinary team. As a member of the team, the nurse should be prepared at the master's or doctoral level in nursing and should be involved in the assessment and planning processes, as well as in care and service coordination (Magyary, Brandt, & Kieckhefer, 2000). Some specific functions in which the advanced practice nurse can contribute to the team include incorporating a family-based approach in early intervention/education services, participating in assessment, developing a plan of care with individual families, coordinating services, advocating, providing direct care, teaching individual families, offering leadership in population-based program planning, conducting program evaluation, designing or implementing research, and being involved in policymaking.

Nursing utilizes a problem-solving method termed the "nursing process," which includes assessment, diagnosis, planning, implementation, and evaluation. During assessment, the nurse gathers data regarding health perceptions and health management practices; nutritional needs; daily activities—sleep-wake patterns, exercise, activity, recreation, vocational pursuits; elimination patterns; cognitive and perceptual functioning; roles, relationships, and social supports; coping and stress responses, including family strengths and resources; self-perception/self-concept; and family and community values, beliefs, concerns, and priorities.

The data collected is used to identify nursing diagnoses or problems in the areas of a child's development, including the physiological and psychosocial realms and his or her education. Nursing diagnoses address the individual's or family's *response* to the health problem, not the actual problem itself. For example, the role of nursing is not to diagnose mental retardation, but rather to address problems that emerge as a result of the medical diagnosis. In providing care for a child with mental retardation, the focus of nursing would be on the parents' understanding of typical developmental milestones and helping them to identify appropriate strategies for behavior support, based on their child's individual level of development.

The unique aspect of nursing is its holistic perspective, whereby the child and his family are viewed as unique beings with physiological, psychological, social, educational, developmental, cultural, and spiritual needs. The nurse does not separate out one aspect of the child or his family, but views each in relationship to the other and within the context of the overall environment.

The ICN supports the position that nurses should be involved in health promotion, education, and counseling programs that serve individuals with disabilities and their families (ICN, 2000). The nurse who specializes in developmental disabilities is responsible for helping individuals achieve their maximal level of health and access available resources to improve their quality of life (Nehring, 1994b).

Possible Challenges for the Professional Nurse on the Team and Strategies To Address These Challenges

Nursing has been involved in the care of individuals with disabilities in the United States since the first mental hospitals (asylums) were built in the 18th century (Nehring, 1994a). Historically, the responsibilities of the nurse have been relatively constant, while the roles have changed from the provision of direct care to these advanced practice roles previously described. As individuals with disabilities have moved from institutional settings to communities and have achieved a higher level of participation in their communities, nurses have adapted to a changing role as team member in a community-based care model (Nehring, 2003). Although nursing has a long history of providing care for individuals with disabilities, the American Nurses Association did not recognize developmental disabilities nursing as a specialty area in the United States until 1997. According to Nehring (2004), this nursing specialty has been stigmatized—much like the population that it serves. Truly, professional nurses who have specialized in this area have shown remarkable dedication to the concept of helping individuals achieve their maximal potential and enjoy a better quality of life.

Interestingly, two issues that were concerns for the profession in the 19th century are still concerns today—education and a shortage of nurses who have been prepared to care for individuals with disabilities (Nehring, 1994a). Traditionally, limited information has been offered in basic nursing education programs about providing health care for individuals with disabilities. Hahn (2003) has indicated a need for greater integration of content related to nursing care of individuals with developmental disabilities into the curricula of basic nursing education programs. In its position statement, *Nursing Education's Agenda for the 21st Century* (1999), the American Association of Colleges of Nursing (AACN) states that "preparation for the entry-level professional nurse now requires a greater orientation to community-based primary health care, and an emphasis on health promotion, maintenance, and cost-effective coordinated care that responds to the needs of culturally diverse groups and underserved and other populations in all settings." Likewise, ICN has taken the position that nursing education programs need to address nursing's role in the prevention of disabilities and the care of persons with disabilities (ICN, 2000).

Most recently, Nehring (2004) has discussed the impact of the current nursing shortage on developmental disabilities nursing. Of particular concern is the decreased number of nurses prepared at the graduate level who are available to coordinate care for the specialty population. This shortage also affects the number of nursing leaders whose responsibility it is to generate and disseminate new nursing knowledge as it relates to the specialty. A continued lack of research and scholarship will affect the advancement of developmental disabilities nursing.

Nehring (2004) has advocated for increasing the number of nurses prepared at the graduate level. The Leadership in Neurodevelopmental and Related Disabilities (LEND) programs, which are funded by the Maternal Child Health Bureau and located at 35 University Centers for Excellence in Developmental Disabilities (UCEDD) located across the United States, are excellent resources. Particularly important is the role of the university nursing faculty member who serves as a liaison to a UCEDD; he or she is able to recruit and mentor nursing graduates who wish to pursue a career in developmental disabilities nursing. Additionally, projects funded by the U.S. Department of Education have served to increase the number of professional nurses who are prepared to serve as members of transdisciplinary teams.

Other issues that the nursing profession must address are education, genetics and biomedical advances, practice guidelines, access to care, quality of care, health care costs, technology, and research (Nehring, 2004). Professional nurses have a continued responsibility to provide leadership in the areas of service provision, research, scholarly publications, education, health policy development, and analysis of emerging ethical issues. Of prime importance is the advancement of this nursing specialty through graduate education, research and scholarship, and mentoring of future leaders.

From a practical standpoint, the most challenging obstacle for the professional nurse as a team member is managing multiple roles, such as coordination of services and the provision of direct care in multiple school settings. Most of the time, the school nurse is responsible for the health maintenance of students at schools within a defined school system, including any special needs children within those schools. Frequently, school nurses must travel to different locations to manage a large caseload of children within the system. As with all professions, the nurse must contend with limited funds and supplies, a jumble of institutional policies and procedures, a variety of personnel, and reimbursement issues. In addition, the nurse usually manages these schools without assistance from any other individual. The health education of the teachers and staff also comes under the responsibility of the school nurse.

Nursing concerns regarding Javier include those that are particular to a child with lumbar spina bifida and hydrocephalus; specifically, the day-to-day management of the child's physical needs. A number of issues must be addressed for children with spina bifida within the program, school, and classroom (Meeropol, 2004; Romanczuk, 2002). These include:

- Providing health education related to a latex-free environment, administration of medications, toileting needs, wound care, urinary catheterization, universal precautions, signs and symptoms of illness (general illness, urinary tract infections, and shunt problems), seizure prevention, signs and symptoms of allergic reaction, emergency procedures, prevention of pressure sores, and cardiopulmonary resuscitation
- Providing health education for all individuals in contact with Javier (e.g., teachers, paraprofessionals, bus drivers, lunchroom staff, office staff, health-room staff)
- Establishing a latex-free environment (classroom, lunchroom, gym/play equipment, housekeeping supplies, school bus, field trip excursions, classroom parties)
- Providing an individualized health plan that includes contact telephone numbers, emergency services with telephone numbers, usual health care provider and telephone number, insurance or health coverage numbers with signed consent to treat forms, individual medication forms and signed consent forms for medication administration, emergency procedures, and names of individuals qualified to manage Javier during the school day
- Providing a safe environment, which includes both transportation and the school setting, and accident prevention.

Summary
The nursing profession addresses the overall health and welfare of individuals with disabilities and their families. The unique aspect of nursing is its holistic perspective, whereby children and family members are viewed as unique beings with physiological, psychological, social, educational, developmental, cultural, and spiritual needs. The nurse provides holistic care, viewing the child and his family within the context of their overall environments.

The profession of nursing has a long history of caring for individuals with disabilities and their families. The roles of caregiver, educator, advocate, counselor, leader/manager, collaborator, change agent, and researcher allow the registered nurse to function as both a direct care provider and a coordinator of care in a variety of settings. The most challenging obstacles for professional nurses who serve as members of transdisciplinary teams include managing numerous roles in multiple settings and working in an environment of strict institutional policies and limited resources.

Issues that continue to challenge nursing include educational preparation and addressing the shortage of professionals who are academically and experientially prepared to serve as members of a transdisciplinary team. The Developmental Disabilities Nurses Association serves to meet the professional needs of nurses in this specialty area and promotes the development of professional expertise. Federally funded programs, such as LEND, are excellent resources for nurses who desire to pursue additional education and acquire clinical experience in the area of developmental disabilities nursing.

References

American Association of Colleges of Nursing. (2004). *Nursing education's agenda for the twenty-first century*. Washington, DC: Author. Retrieved August 17, 2004, from www.aacn.nche.edu/Publications/positions/nrsgedag.htm.

American Nurses Association. (2004). *Member benefits*. Washington, DC: Author. Retrieved August 17, 2004, from www.nursingworld.org/member2.htm

Developmental Disabilities Nurses Association. www.ddna.org

Hahn, J. E. (2003). Addressing the need for education: Curriculum development for nurses about intellectual and development disabilities. *Nursing Clinics of North America, 38*(2), 185-204.

International Council of Nurses. (2000). *Prevention of disability and the care of people with disabilities*. Geneva, Switzerland: Author. Retrieved August 17, 2004, from www.icn.ch/psdisability00.htm.

International Council of Nurses. (2004). *The ICN definition of nursing*. Geneva, Switzerland: Author. Retrieved August 17, 2004, from www.icn.ch/.

Magyary, D., Brandt, P., & Kieckhefer, G. (2000). The nursing role within an interdisciplinary assessment team. In M. J. Guralnick (Ed.), *Interdisciplinary clinical assessment of young children with developmental disabilities* (pp. 85-103). Baltimore: Brookes.

Meeropol, E. (2004). Latex allergy in 2004: What's known, what's now, what's next. *Insights, 15*(4), 6-7.

Morse, J. S. (1994). An overview of developmental disabilities nursing. In S. P. Roth & J. S. Morse (Eds.), *A life-span approach to nursing care for individuals with developmental disabilities* (pp. 19-58). Baltimore: Brookes.

Nehring, W. M. (1994a). A history of nursing in developmental disabilities in America. In S. P. Roth & J. S. Morse (Eds.), *A life-span approach to nursing care for individuals with developmental disabilities* (pp. 1-18). Baltimore: Brookes.

Nehring, W. M. (1994b). The nurse whose specialty is developmental disabilities. *Pediatric Nursing, 20*(1), 78-81.

Nehring, W. M. (2003). History of the roles of nurses caring for persons with mental retardation. *Nursing Clinics of North America, 38*(2), 351-372.

Nehring, W. M. (2004, April 16). Directions for the future of intellectual and developmental disabilities as a nursing specialty. *International Journal of Nursing in Intellectual and Developmental Disabilities, 1*(1), Article 2. Retrieved August 13, 2004, from www.journal.hsmc.org/ijnidd.

Romanczuk, A. N. (2002). What teachers need to know: The ABC's of spina bifida. *Insights Into Spina Bifida, 13*(4), 5A & 8A.

Chapter 10

WHAT OTHERS SHOULD KNOW ABOUT ENGLISH LANGUAGE LEARNER (ELL) PROFESSIONALS

Anarella Cellitti & Jerry Aldridge

The primary role of English Language Learner (ELL) professionals is to facilitate communication and understanding between the family and child and the team. The ELL specialist can come from many disciplines. She can be an educator, a social worker, or a trained community worker. The key for these personnel is the ability to understand the language, as well as the cultural issues faced by the population they are serving (Lynch & Hanson, 2004). In some states, an English as a Second Language (ESL) certificate is all that is required to become a specialist. In most cases, the ELL specialist is not required to be bilingual, which presents a major problem in communicating with the family and the child.

Ideally, the ELL specialist should speak the language of the family she is serving. Special attention must be placed on the degree of bilingualism. When a child with special needs is involved, extensive bilingualism is necessary due to the nature of the services required. It is also important that the specialist be able to read and write proficiently in both languages, in light of the fact that she may need to translate written information for the family and the school. In addition, the person should be familiar with possible variations of the language according to the different populations. The version of Spanish spoken by Mexicans can vary significantly from the ones spoken by other Latin American communities. If the translator is unfamiliar with colloquialisms, serious misunderstandings can occur and lead to misinterpretations of treatment procedures.

Another critical factor to consider with ELL personnel is cultural training and sensitivity (Green, 1999). Many bilingual individuals, however well-intentioned, do not have the multicultural perspective necessary for working with diverse groups. A well-trained ELL member should be educated in specific cultural practices and maintain an attitude of respect and acceptance towards them. Emphasis should be placed on selecting an ecocultural framework, wherein the team analyzes the family unit by understanding the specifics of the family events, beliefs and values, patterns of behavior, family composition, and the physical setting in which the family lives. Generalizations about the family should be avoided, even though the specialist needs an understanding of the larger cultural context (Harry, 2002).

Roles and Contributions of English Language Learner Personnel on the Team

ELL professionals should have a general background of the cultural history, customs, traditions, and lifestyles of the families with whom they work, and be able to explain this knowledge to other members of the team. Although it is important to understand that Javier, the child presented in the case study in Chapter 3, is from Mexico, we need to know more specifics about where in Mexico he is from. A child from Chiapas may be different than a child from Mexico City or any of the border towns. Each region of Mexico has specific values, beliefs, and cultural practices concerning family structures, power structures, and disabilities. The

second language

Mexican population includes many different ethnic groups. A family may be from a particular region but belong to a distinct indigenous group. An ELL consultant will research this information and share it with the team so a clear view of the child and family emerges before interventions begin.

The ELL professional needs to be fully aware of the differences in child-rearing practices that can benefit or impede the treatment plan. For example, many Latin American countries do not place a priority on encouraging children's autonomy. Parents may dress, feed, and do others things for their children even though the child may be old enough or physically able to do so on his own. A well-trained ELL consultant will explain this dynamic to the team. Understanding the relevant child-rearing practices and parent-child relationships can be beneficial in setting goals/outcomes and objectives/strategies that do not contradict the parents' cultural values. For example, Javier's parents allow him to have temper tantrums without any consequences. Part of the issue is that Javier's family believes that he is unable to control his behavior due his disability, and so the expectation is that the parents, siblings, relatives, and friends will exercise patience. When addressing this issue with the parents, presenting it as a "social acceptance" matter—in other words, Javier would have an easier time being accepted by his peers if he did not have so many tantrums—may help the family understand and appreciate the team's concerns. In addition, out of concern for Javier, the team would have to address the family's discipline strategies, because physical punishment is a common practice among many Latino families.

Sensitive ELL practitioners will educate parents about behavioral changes and treatment implementation in culturally appropriate ways. Family practices, such as discipline, are often delicate to address. In general, corporal punishment is a common and accepted practice in Mexico. Certain practices, such as making children kneel on rice or sending them to sleep without food, may be socially acceptable. Therefore, the team members would need to discuss legal concerns about these practices, while suggesting other ways to redirect children's behavior. Team members, in their discussions with parents, should emphasize that they are not judging the family's cultural practices. Nevertheless, the family does need to be informed that these practices are considered abusive in the United States and can have legal ramifications. In addition, the ELL professional can explain certain behavior support strategies through role-play. We can teach parents behavior support techniques if we understand the child's roles and family's values. Be careful in selecting strategies, as techniques that give children equal status with the parents and allow children to select their own consequences for misbehavior may not be culturally appropriate.

Possible Challenges for English Language Learner Personnel on the Team and Strategies To Address These Challenges

Team members also must consider how different cultures view children with disabilities. The cultural view of disabilities varies within countries. The fact is that in many Latin American countries, people with disabilities are not included in many aspects of society. Many Mexican families may not have been exposed to role models of successfully and fully functioning individuals who have a particular disability. Parents or guardians may have unrealistic expectations (high or low) concerning intervention.

Parents from some parts of Mexico may work to make the child less autonomous and the focus or center of family life an approach that generally is not viewed as appropriate in the United States. Also, the parents of children with disabilities tend to feel undue shame and responsibility for the disability. In this case, the team needs to spend some time helping Javier's family understand that his challenges were not the result of improper parenting. Particularly, Javier's father may benefit from discussing the fact that Javier's problems do not reflect upon his manhood or ability to procreate loving children. Latino males tend to internalize their child's disability as a failure; consequently, they may suggest or encourage withdrawal from treatment. It is obvious that Javier's father has distanced himself from the care of his son. The treatment team needs to consider whether this is due to the typical Latino perception that the responsibility for child care lies with the mother or if this is due to internalized shame and/or guilt.

Again, it is important to emphasize that in many Latino groups, women are expected to take care of children, particularly when the children are sick or have a disability. In many Latino cultures, children often have a high status in a family, often higher than for spouses. A child who has special needs often assumes a more important role. The mother's role is also different and she sees herself doing more for her children. Self-sacrifice is considered a positive value and is encouraged as a cultural trait. The ELL professional will need to work with families to convey the importance of allowing the child to be as functional as possible. Therefore, the team has to carefully address the need for Javier to be self-sufficient at school and other settings. If the team members address the need for Javier to be autonomous at home, they risk alienating the family. Family members could perceive such statements as attempts to minimize their role in helping Javier.

With regard to Javier, the role of the extended family is another consideration. Many Latinos live with grandparents and/or aunts and uncles. All of these adults have input in the child-rearing practices of the home. Therefore, in order to preserve the integrity of the family structure, all of the adults need to have their voices heard. The ELL teacher should help the team include as many family members as the family desires in team meetings, discussions, and decisions. Also, the team should allow time for all these family members to participate if they wish to do so, and have someone to negotiate among family members if their views about interventions differ. Such tensions could not only limit support for the child but also jeopardize family cohesion.

Families' power structures also need to be determined and understood. In many families, the husband and wife share decision-making power, but this may not be the case in a Mexican family. Mexican women from families of lower socioeconomic status often have little or no control over certain aspects of family life. Their male partners are the ones who make decisions, including those concerning their children. It is imperative that ELL personnel use care when asking questions, directing them to both parents and/or family members. Also, observations during meetings can be used to determine the power roles within the family, watching for indicators such as the female deferring decisions to the male or not speaking until the male partner speaks. If this is the case, the team should never put the female in the role of making a decision without consulting her partner, since this can have serious negative consequences for her.

Uninformed personnel commonly ask children (e.g., older siblings) to act as translators. This practice is inappropriate for several reasons. One is the obvious possibility of getting an inaccurate translation due to a child's limited vocabulary. A more serious problem concerns the family's power structure. Children in Latino families typically are not included in family decisions. They hold a very "child-like" place in the family; to ask them to translate involves them in "adult" issues and gives them power over the adults, which is not culturally appropriate. The ELL professionals need to discourage team members from engaging in such a practice, as it is likely to create friction between children and parents. In addition, issues of loyalty and status may arise if a friend is used to translate what team members are saying.

The best solution is to hire a translator who has no personal ties to the family and can offer objective information and feedback—something that may be difficult to do when dealing with a family friend. Using a professional translator and/or interpreter also can ensure that the information is properly translated and that no misunderstandings occur. In addition, this practice can reduce the possibility of legal actions in the future if something happens to the child as a result of miscommunication.

In order for an effective team to work with immigrant children, it is essential that team members address their personal viewpoints about immigration. There often is a climate of xenophobia underlying discussions about immigration among people born in the United States. In addition, some people believe that immigrants should work hard, cause no problems, stay quiet, act "properly" (meaning the way Anglo Americans do), and require no social services. If members of the team betray such anti-immigration feelings, they need to be discussed openly in the team's meetings. The fact that Javier's parents are undocumented workers could generate some negative feelings within the team. The team leader needs to be alert for this possibility, and intervene and/or remove any member who is unable to deal with this issue.

Also, Javier's family may believe that because of their immigration status, they have forfeited their rights to receive particular services. The family may be afraid of deportation, and they may be unaware of the services available for the child and family regardless of their undocumented status. The ELL consultant needs to inform the family of immigration policies at the local, state, and federal levels, and act as an advocate on their behalf.

As undocumented immigrants commonly mistrust "the system" and fear being reported, the team needs to be aware of and patient about a family's likely attempts to "test" the team members' loyalty and support, and to question the validity of information being given. It may work best for the team to select only one member to distribute verbal or written information to all the different family members, making sure to provide consistent answers in order to minimize mistrust and misunderstanding.

A well-trained ELL team member understands all issues related to immigration and acculturation, including stages of, and common reactions to, immigration. They will have knowledge about the causes and consequences of cultural shock, and can educate the rest of the team members about it. They also will be aware of the psychological concerns related to immigration, such as the behaviors and feelings that put individuals at risk for social rejection and misunderstanding, causes and stages of loss, depression, and feeling estranged from the new culture. These syndromes associated with immigration can be discussed in team meetings.

Finally, the family's socioeconomic status must be taken into account. If immigrant families come from a middle class background, chances are that their language skills will be more advanced (in their primary language, as well as in English), therefore making the ELL professional's job easier. If the family is from a lower socioeconomic stratum, however, they may have more difficulty understanding the terminology, and so the ELL consultant will have to spend more time making sure that the family really understands the information. Literacy even in the primary language cannot be assumed, and so efforts should be made to discuss any written information to clarify understanding.

As much as possible, the treatment plan must not be ethnocentric (Sue & Sue, 1990). In general, the approach to intervention in the United States reflects white, middle-class values. Immigrant families may be guarded when interacting with clinicians (Sue & Sue, 1990). In addition, if interventions are used that are too culturally different and parents feel pressure to participate in behaviors foreign to them, the team has simply become another oppressor of the family.

In addition, ELL personnel need to understand that if openness occurs with the team, it will be within the context of the culture. The family may assume a closer relationship than the members of the team may feel comfortable with. The family may consider team members as a part of the "family," and treat them as such. Some members of the team may find such behavior inappropriate. Javier's parents may expect the team members to spend some time talking about other family members or community events before talking "business." Latinos, in general, place a lot of importance on this "social talk." It is perceived as a sign of interest in the person; therefore, if it is absent, it will put the family on the defensive and leave them feeling devalued by the team. The team needs to allow time in their schedule to engage in this kind of verbal and social interaction in order to maintain good communication and rapport with Javier's family. In addition, many Latinos would expect that the team members will eat proffered food during the home visit and respond positively to other overtures of hospitality, no matter how much these behaviors may be considered inappropriate in the mainstream culture of the United States.

The ELL consultant will have to navigate this issue, assuring the team that it may be necessary for them to venture outside of their emotional and social comfort zone in order to work with the family. On the other hand, if this closeness becomes an intolerable issue, the ELL person may need to address such concerns with the family. There are trade-offs to doing this; it can help the family become more socially appropriate but also may alienate them from the team. Team members will have to assess the situation and the people involved before deciding how to proceed.

Another cultural factor in interventions and services in the United States is the emphasis on keeping physical, religious, and psychological components separate (Sue & Sue, 1990); this can be another cause for cultural misunderstanding and intervention failure. Many Mexican families have a strong Catholic/Christian faith. Sometimes, they may follow such folkloric beliefs as the "mal de ojo" (i.e., belief in the evil eye, or someone putting a curse on them). Some believe in alternative treatments to induce healing (e.g., herbs, spiritual treatments) (Applewhite, 1995). The ELL consultant should be able to understand this belief system and work with the family without passing judgment.

Javier's family is planning for a visit to the Basilica de Guadalupe in Mexico City, and may be devoting their financial resources to do so. The team may need to process their feelings about this issue, since Javier's family is placing great emphasis on making the trip. The team might benefit from talking to the family priest and getting his perspective prior to the trip. Team members must carefully monitor their comments related to the possibility of a cure, and offer acceptance as long as Javier's early intervention treatment is not interrupted. This issue is extremely important, since many parents may refuse or discontinue interventions if they sense that their beliefs are not being respected.

Another cultural issue concerns differences in orientation to time. Many Americans are future-oriented, while many Latinos (particularly, Mexicans) are past- and present-oriented. Therefore, Javier's family may be more responsive to interventions that have immediate influences on the child. Furthermore, the immediate needs of family and friends may take precedence over transdisciplinary team meetings. It is important to remember the family is not deliberately attempting to antagonize the team.

One last point to remember is that many of the characteristics displayed by the Gonzales family can be explained in relation to socioeconomic status. Several of the behaviors seen in Javier's family correspond to behaviors typically associated with poverty (Payne, 1996). The team members need to understand that culture, socioeconomic status, and gender are interrelated issues that cannot be addressed separately. The members of the team can benefit from additional education concerning economic patterns as well as their own biases and expectations about poverty. Without this careful analysis of variables affecting a particular family, the effectiveness of interventions will be limited at best.

References

Applewhite, S. L. (1995). Curanderismo: Demystifying the health beliefs and practices of elderly Mexican Americans. *Health & Social Work, 20,* 247-253.

Greene, M. S. (1999). A parent's perspective: A response to G. Mahoney and others. *Topics in Early Childhood Special Education, 19*(3), 149-151.

Harry, B. (2002). *Cultural diversity, families, and the special education system: Communication and empowerment.* New York: Teachers College Press.

Lynch, E. W., & Hanson, M. J. (2004). *Developing cross-cultural competence: A guide for working with children and their families* (3rd ed.). Baltimore: Brookes.

Payne, J. L. (1996). Absence of judgment: What social workers believe about the poor will hamper welfare reform. *Policy Review, 80,* 50-54.

Sue, D. W., & Sue, D. (1990). *Counseling the culturally different: Theory and practice* (2nd ed.). New York: Wiley-Interscience.

Chapter 11

MAKING TRANSDISCIPLINARY TEAMING WORK: PULLING IT ALL TOGETHER

— Jerry Aldridge

As we have seen throughout the past chapters, transdisciplinary teaming is one of the most challenging and rewarding experiences professionals face in early intervention/education. This chapter will examine four important questions related to transdisciplinary teaming: 1) What makes transdisciplinary teaming work? 2) What are some issues facing teams today? 3) What are some other scenarios or cases to consider? and 4) What new challenges do teams face?

What Makes Transdisciplinary Teaming Work?

Many factors contribute to effective transdisciplinary teaming. However, most of them fall under one of the following elements or characteristics of effective teams:

There Is Continuous Communication. While communication may begin with the team meetings, ongoing communication is required that extends beyond the time frame of team meetings. Effective team members are continually sharing information; describing their interventions, successes, and failures; and seeking feedback from one another. While time is an issue for most teams, there are many ways to make continual communication possible, including E-mail, voice mail, cell phones, and other. The importance of communicating with the family as vital team members cannot be overstated. We have seen in the Gonzales case study the family's need to communicate with other team members and their interest in taking care of Javier in school. The family's desire to gain a cure for Javier through a pilgrimage and their ideas about discipline and how to deal with Javier's tantrums also were communicated in order to develop the most appropriate individual education plan for Javier.

Quality Programs Are in Place. Effective teamwork can be accomplished more easily in high-quality programs. This means that the professional members of the team are well-grounded in recommended practices. When quality programs are not implemented, a domino effect occurs, as in the following example. A kindergarten teacher insists that the children in her room write the letters of the alphabet on lined paper. This is done "out of context," which means that the children work on skills that are isolated and have no meaning to them and no relevance to their everyday lives. In this class, students are expected to make a line of "e's," using two-finger spacing; this would be considered a developmentally inappropriate activity. Meanwhile, the kindergarten teacher enlists the help of the occupational therapist and the physical therapist to support a child with severe cerebral palsy with the writing assignment. In essence, she asks for their assistance with an activity that is inappropriate for the child. Although the physical therapist and the occupational therapist work closely with the teacher to assist the child, they are unfamiliar with developmentally appropriate practice and, therefore, do not realize that the writing activity is inappropriate. While the team communicates effectively and works well together, the quality of instruction is questionable. In this example, the team has collaborated to provide inappropriate instruction. This program was not high quality because the general educator was not knowledgeable in appropriate prac-

integration

tices of her professional discipline; therefore, the team was ineffective. Quality programs are indeed central to effective teamwork.

Team Members Are Well-prepared. For teams to work effectively, personnel preparation at multiple levels is necessary. First, team members must be knowledgeable and up-to-date in their respective fields. In the previous example, team members who were well-prepared in their respective disciplines would have been able to provide a program of higher quality. In addition, team members should know a considerable amount about the other disciplines represented on the teams. Team members also should be prepared with regard to the family and culture. While it is not possible to know every family structure, culture, and context particular to the children we serve, team members are responsible for finding out as much as possible about the family and culture before the team meetings. Yet, sometimes parents, children, and family members do not subscribe to the values that we have researched regarding their primary culture. Team members who are well-prepared can inquire, "I read this about the Latino culture. Can you tell me if this is important to you?" While team members should be well-prepared, they also should be flexible. New information will often change the course of intervention, which makes flexibility the key to success.

All Team Members Teach, Learn, and Work Together. Respect and equal partnership for all team members are necessary components in order to provide services together and to teach, learn, and develop programs together. This requires sharing of information, listening, questioning, and working toward a consensus. A transdisciplinary team member brings individual knowledge, skills, information, and preparedness to the table, but goals and objectives are jointly negotiated. Administrative support and encouragement also are vital elements in the process.

There Is a Willingness To Share Information and Knowledge. Team members will use discipline-specific information that is salient for decision-making as they teach, learn, and work together. For transdisciplinary teaming to work, all team members must be open to finding and sharing information. One example related to Javier involved the physical therapist's willingness to communicate with the other physical therapists who provide services at the state rehabilitation agency's spina bifida clinic. After the physical therapist gathered the information, she shared it with the team so that pertinent medical and equipment issues could be incorporated into the planning for Javier's kindergarten experience.

Team Members Cross Disciplinary Boundaries. As team members jointly develop goals/outcomes and objectives/strategies, they consider the best ways to deliver services. This means that the early childhood special educator might conduct circle time or work with the entire kindergarten class, while the general educator focuses specifically on a child with special needs or observes the child's interactions with peers. Service delivery is well-planned and coordinated, and team members bring cutting-edge recommendations to the table. During implementation of the planned service, professional boundaries are often blurred. The occupational therapist cannot be in the same kindergarten class every day to work with Javier; however, the OT can teach the general education teacher how to implement the jointly agreed upon modifications.

There Is an Extra Effort Made To Develop a Partnership With the Family Members or Caregivers. Such teaming models as multidisciplinary or interdisciplinary incorporate the family into the team. In those models, however, the specialists often tell family members what they think is best. With transdisciplinary teaming, professionals make special efforts to work collaboratively with the family members, listen to them, and incorporate their issues, hopes, dreams, and concerns into action. This was particularly true in Javier's case. While the parents' goal of taking care of Javier and their ideas concerning a pilgrimage for healing were different from the rest of the team members' ideas, these goals were considered and respected. Negotiations addressed how to provide culturally appropriate, individually appropriate, and age-appropriate goals and objectives for Javier.

There Is an Emphasis on the Natural Environment. In the past, "pull-out programs" were rampant for the delivery of services to children with special needs. Communication specialists, occupational therapists, speech-language pathologists, and early interventionists pulled children from their regular programs to deliver isolated services. By contrast, transdisciplinary services require services to be implemented in the natural environment whenever possible. For example, feeding support occurs during lunch and snack time, and a child's mobility needs are met through naturally occurring movement opportunities in the classroom, school, and community.

Ideally, transdisciplinary team members receive joint training in conflict resolution techniques. Conflicts are natural events for transdisciplinary teams. Consensus building and compromise are necessary to provide the best possible situation in which to provide learning opportunities and support.

What Are Some Issues Facing Teams Today?

Throughout the earlier chapters, we have described numerous obstacles that teams may face. In summary, we can focus on eight general issues facing teams: 1) lack of time, 2) different philosophical approaches, 3) personality conflicts, 4) lack of administrative support, 5) lack of knowledge concerning appropriate practice, 6) lack of trust, 7) team members who advocate practices in conflict with the family's cultural values, and 8) the general education teacher's resistance. For each issue, we offer suggestions for moving beyond the issue and toward finding a solution.

There Is Not Enough Time. Perhaps the number one problem facing transdisciplinary teams today is the lack of time needed to plan and implement services as a team. Scheduling conflicts, heavy case loads, other responsibilities, and family availability all work against transdisciplinary teaming. To help alleviate some of the time constraints, the following are needed:

- Administrative support and coordination
- Flexibility in scheduling
- Team members who "think outside the box" in order to find creative ways to meet.

Team Members Have Vastly Different Philosophical Approaches to Service Delivery. As McLaren (2003) points out, education is never neutral. There is always a philosophical basis for making decisions, whether implicit or explicit. A major problem occurs when professionals and families approach education and services from differing philosophical or ideological viewpoints. These differences can be quite complex and multidimensional. For example, the general early childhood teacher may approach teaching from a behavioral perspective, while the early childhood special education teacher could approach instruction from a constructivist framework. Compounding the differences in approaches would be ideological considerations related to how services should be delivered. For example, the general early childhood education teacher may prefer all support to be delivered in the regular classroom, but the speech-language pathologist could push for a pull-out model of service delivery. To help deal with these issues, readers may want to consider the following recommendations:

- Each team member should openly discuss her philosophical and ideological beliefs related to planning, assessment, and service delivery. This provides the team members with a frame of reference about how each member approaches decisions.
- Each team member should respect different philosophical approaches, with the goal

of working together in the best interests of the children involved. A philosophical viewpoint is neither true nor false and, therefore, cannot be clearly debated. Different team members interpret the world in different ways. Accepting the views of others can help team members move beyond theoretical arguments and instead consider the best ways to implement services, realizing there will be differences of opinion.

Personality Conflicts Often Occur. Every member of the team will have strengths and weaknesses in terms of his or her contribution to the team. Some team members see the big picture but are not concerned with details. Others like things orderly and specific and prefer looking at the parts rather than the whole. These differences inevitably lead to personality conflicts. To work through this, the following suggestions are made:

- The team may want to purchase and read the book *Please Understand Me* (2000) by David Keirsey and Marilyn Bates. This book describes 16 personality types and how to best work with each type.
- In extreme cases, in order to avoid domination of the group by certain team members, it might be appropriate to develop specific rules for interaction. For example, one rule might be, "Each person will describe the goals he or she believes to be important for Javier before we discuss them."

Administrative Support Is Often Lacking. Administrative support might not be available for many reasons. Lack of knowledge on the administrator's part, time constraints, and other priorities are a few examples. While we cannot make a "silk purse out of a sow's ear," there are things the team can do to promote better administrative support. A few suggestions include:

- Plan a team meeting with the administrator, with all members of the team in attendance if possible.
- Develop specific goals/objectives for the meeting with administrator(s), requesting the particular type of supports the team needs to do its work.
- As a team, approach the administrator(s) with the agenda and present a positive, united front on behalf of the children and families served.

Administrators can take a number of steps to facilitate the implementation of a transdisciplinary model. Table 11.1 provides a list of suggestions for administrators.

There Is a Lack of Knowledge Concerning Appropriate Practice. It is understandable that each team member may not be proficient or competent at first in the recommended practices for each of the represented disciplines. As the team works together over time, however, recommended practices in each of the represented disciplines can be approached by:

- Sharing recommended practice guidelines, such as *DEC Recommended Practices for Early Intervention/Early Childhood Special Education* (Sandall, Hemmeter, Smith, & McLean, 2005) and *Developmentally Appropriate Practice in Early Childhood Programs* (Bredekamp & Copple, 1997), with all team members.
- Having an open discussion about issues related to the delivery of recommended practices. For example, most states in the United States have guidelines about the role of nursing in school programs and what teachers and paraprofessionals are allowed (and not allowed) to do. It will be important, particularly in Javier's case, for the nurse to be well-versed in these practices and to share the information with the other team members.

There Is Often a Lack of Trust Among Team Members. This lack of trust may be especially true of the family members. Remember that in Javier's case, his parents continually asked for the same information from various team members. Their precarious status as undocumented immigrants added to their distrust. Parents, however, are not the only team members who may have trust issues. To develop trust among team members, it is important to keep in mind the following suggestions:

- The team should deal with the issue of trust as directly and as openly as possible. The team leader should monitor communications by asking frequently, "Do we have any issues related to feeling comfortable with this process?" or "What concerns do you have that you might be hesitant to discuss?" The team leader should model this trust and demonstrate that he or she can be trusted.
- Make a special effort to work on the trust issue with the family representatives. Team members can plan to call the family from time to time to ask, "How are things going?" or "Is there anything you need from the team?"

Team Members May Advocate Practices That Are in Conflict With the Family's Cultural Values. If team members are unfamiliar with the family's culture, this could happen without the awareness of many team members. For instance, in Javier's case, the family does not want Javier to be independent until he is older, a dynamic that is true in many Latino cultures for typically developing children. However, the issue is exacerbated

---

Steps Administrators Can Take To Facilitate Implementation of a Transdisciplinary Approach

- Encourage individual professionals to view themselves as responsible to the team.
- Encourage the team to view itself as responsible to the child and the family.
- Encourage involvement of parents at whatever level they choose to participate.
- Arrange program/school schedules to allow for formal, general staff meetings.
- Model appropriate behavior in team meetings (e.g., active listening, support).
- Arrange the program/school building to maximize interactions between children with and without disabilities.
- Arrange the building and schedule to avoid reliance on separate therapy rooms.
- Encourage teachers and related services personnel to work together to assess children's strengths and needs and to develop goals and objectives.
- Encourage a data-based model of instruction.
- Encourage the use of clear, simple language in meetings, IEPs, reports, and discussions.
- Do not attempt to prevent conflict, but help resolve it as it arises.
- Give the transdisciplinary model time to work.

Table 11.1

when Javier's physical challenges are added as well as his parents' cautious and protective behavior. Team members need to completely understand the cultural influences in order to recommend culturally appropriate practices. To better accommodate the family's cultural background, the following recommendations are made:

- The team members could discuss the family's beliefs and the school's practices—especially when they are in conflict. For example, Javier looks down when his parents call his name, having been taught to do so out of respect. His teacher, however, may say, "Javier, look at me when I am talking to you."
- The team could discuss with the family the possibility of helping the child to "code switch." In code switching, the child is taught to respond one way at home and another way at school.
- The team could discuss with the family their preference that Javier respond in school the same way he is expected to respond at home. These negotiations would encourage the parents to see themselves as active members of the team and participants in their child's education.

The General Education Teacher May Not Want Therapists in the Classroom. Remember, teachers who graduated from college many years ago most likely were taught that they were responsible for their own classroom, rather than it being a joint responsibility of a team of individuals. New teachers also may be territorial of their classroom, because they may not feel confident enough of their own skills and abilities as teachers and may be cautious about being "on display" when others come into "their" classrooms. Ideas for addressing this issue include:

- The team could discuss these concerns openly and honestly with the general education teacher. They might ask, "What concerns do you have with therapists coming into the classroom?" Often, the problem centers around the time frame in which a therapist is able to provide services. The general education teacher may be concerned about disruptions in the classroom.
- The team should negotiate and develop a plan for service delivery in the natural setting, listening carefully and respecting the general educator's point of view.

What Are Some Other Scenarios or Cases To Consider?

So far, we have focused on the case of Javier as an example of how transdisciplinary teaming works. Many other scenarios are likely, however. Here are seven other examples of transdisciplinary issues. Based on Javier's example and also what you have learned thus far from this book, how would you approach each of the following cases in your respective discipline and as a member of a transdisciplinary team?

1. Jamal and Sara are 4-year-old fraternal twins. Both have mild cerebral palsy. However, Sara has more issues related to gross and fine motor functioning. Their parents come from a country/culture in which men are respected more than women. An occupational therapist works with several children at the preschool the children attend. The occupational therapist and Jamal's and Sara's teacher have referred both Jamal and Sara for evaluation. They believe that both might benefit from occupational and/or physical therapy. The father has agreed for Jamal, the son, to be evaluated, but does not agree to have Sara tested. What would you do? Why?

2. Maria is a child from Mexico attending a public school kindergarten in a rural area of the United States. The kindergarten teacher believes in a constructivist approach and works

toward developing autonomy, as quickly as possible, for the children in her classroom. Maria has arthrogryposis, meaning she was born with multiple joint contractures in all her limbs. The occupational therapist has worked diligently to develop an assistive device to help Maria during mealtime. Maria's mother comes to kindergarten during lunch time several days a week and insists on feeding her. She, as part of her cultural background, believes that other adults also should feed Maria until she is older. What would you do? Why?

3. Mr. Vance is a speech-language pathologist and Ms. Katz is a physical therapist. They are both near retirement and were educated in their respective disciplines over 30 years ago. The general early childhood programs in which they work strongly encourage full inclusion of students with disabilities. However, Mr. Vance and Ms. Katz have been resistant to that philosophy. Both believe they are being quite reasonable when pulling each child away from the other children in the regular classroom to administer therapy in isolation. If you were the general or special education teacher, what would you do?

4. Jessica is in the 1st grade. Her teacher, Ms. Ward, is quite traditional and insists that Jessica learn to write on lined paper and stay within the lines. Ms. Ward directs the children to practice writing letters of the alphabet in isolation every day. For example, each child is expected to write the letter "e" on lined paper, using two-finger spacing. The occupational therapist has worked hard to prepare modifications for Jessica's writing exercises. The early childhood special education teacher, however, believes this practice is not realistic, not in context, and developmentally inappropriate. If you were the early childhood special education teacher, what would you do?

5. In one school district, the transdisciplinary team members are remarkable. They work together and are truly committed to open communication, serving children and families to the best of their abilities, resolving conflicts, and, for lack of a better phrase, "being all they can be." However, the therapists have too many schools to visit, too many children to serve adequately, and no time to accomplish even half of what they could with fewer case loads. What can be done about this?

6. Ms. Echols is a traditional preschool teacher. She believes that her classroom is "HER classroom" and does NOT want transdisciplinary team members in her classroom. What might be some of the reasons for Ms. Echols' reluctance to have additional personnel in her room? What could the team members do to work with Ms. Echols and the children and families in this class?

7. Lydia has cerebral palsy and is blind. Mr. Sims, her 1st-grade teacher, is very committed to including Lydia in class. However, his class is quite challenging. He has two children who are prone to violent behavior and he is terrified that a child will hurt Lydia. The problem is compounded because Lydia is not toilet trained. What can team members do to meet Lydia's needs and also work to help Mr. Sims become a supportive teacher and advocate for Lydia?

What New Challenges Do Teams Face?

As transdisciplinary teams navigate together with parents and professionals to meet the challenges of today, other obstacles arise as if to test our ability to develop and deliver transdisciplinary services. One important example that has risen in the past few years in the United States is the No Child Left Behind Act of 2001. Children in special education are now expected to take standardized tests with limited or no modifications. Many general and special educators believe this runs counter to recommended practice; yet, they are obligated to meet the guidelines of No Child Left Behind. This presents a plethora of new challenges for transdisciplinary teams. These challenges will mean additional training for professionals and pre-professionals entering the service professions.

References

Bredekamp, S., & Copple, C. (Eds.). (1997). *Developmentally appropriate practice in early childhood programs* (Rev. ed.). Washington, DC: National Association for the Education of Young Children.

Keirsey, D., & Bates, M. (2000). *Please understand me.* New York: Free Press.

McLaren, P. (2003). *Life in schools: An introduction to critical pedagogy in the foundations of education* (4th ed.). Boston: Allyn & Bacon.

No Child Left Behind Act of 2001. (PL 107-110)

Sandall, S., Hemmeter, M. L., Smith, B. J. , & McLean, M. E. (Eds.). (2005). *DEC recommended practices: A comprehensive guide for practical application in early intervention/early childhood special education* (2nd ed.). Longmont, CO: Sopris West.

Chapter 12

TRANSDISCIPLINARY TEAMING FROM A HIGHER EDUCATION PERSPECTIVE

Jennifer L. Kilgo

Early intervention/education team members from across disciplines need both preservice and inservice preparation that provides them with skills in inclusive practices, collaboration, consultation, co-teaching, and working as members of transdisciplinary teams (Stayton, Miller, & Dinnebeil, 2005). Many professionals lack the skills needed to collaborate effectively as transdisciplinary team members alongside professionals from other disciplines (Stayton, Miller, & Dinnebeil, 2002). Many of those involved in higher education advocate for an integrated approach to personnel preparation, one that recognizes the knowledge bases of general early childhood education, early childhood special education, and related service disciplines (Kilgo & Bruder, 1997). However, Bailey (1996) summarized several studies indicating that graduate programs spend little time on team processes, with virtually no experience in the context of transdisciplinary teams. In recent years, the call has gone out to increase the emphasis on teaming skills in personnel preparation programs at both the preservice and inservice levels (Kilgo & Bruder, 1997; Miller & Stayton, 2005).

Although the momentum of the past decade has led to the availability of inclusive educational environments for young children, these programs often have been staffed by teachers and therapists prepared in traditional discipline-specific programs. Many colleges and universities across the United States are responding to the changes in early childhood environments by redesigning their personnel preparation programs to reflect transdisciplinary team-based practices (Kilgo & Bruder, 1997; Miller & Stayton, 2005; Stayton et al., 2002). The example below illustrates how one urban university has met the challenge of developing a transdisciplinary graduate training program.

Faculty members representing multiple disciplines and departments at the University of Alabama at Birmingham (UAB) have worked together for many years to design dynamic experiences to prepare graduate students for transdisciplinary service delivery. In 1999 and again in 2004, UAB received personnel preparation grants from the U.S. Department of Education to develop and implement a master's-level preservice preparation program. This program is designed to increase the quantity, quality, and diversity of personnel who provide services to young children with disabilities and their families. Students from early childhood special education, general early childhood, physical therapy, occupational therapy, speech-language pathology, and nursing gain transdisciplinary team experience through seminars and field experiences. Team learning is promoted as students and faculty members work together, share expertise, and collaborate to serve young children with low-incidence disabilities and their families. The benefits of transdisciplinary personnel preparation are numerous, as described in Table 12.1.

The program at UAB is based on the belief that young children with disabilities and their families require teams of professionals from diverse backgrounds who are well-prepared with skills in transdisciplinary teamwork, collaboration, family-centered and culturally sensitive approaches, instructional and assistive technology, and effective strategies for promoting inclusion. Seminars have been designed to

higher education

Benefits of a Transdisciplinary Approach
to Personnel Preparation

Training Programs
* Draws on the expertise of faculty from various disciplines across the college or university
* Develops transdisciplinary content, processes, and experiences
* Infuses content into existing courses across departments
* Provides for continuity in instructional content and procedures across departments
* Assists in collaboratively meeting state-wide personnel needs and shortages
* Helps in modifying and meeting certification and licensure requirements across disciplines
* Increases visibility and impact within the community, college or university, and state

Faculty Members
* Provides access to instructional resources across disciplines
* Encourages the exchange of information across disciplines (e.g., state and federal initiatives, personnel shortages, recommended practices)
* Builds alliances across disciplines to promote and achieve mutual objectives
* Provides a forum for issues and ideas among professional peers with similar interests
* Facilitates collegial support among faculty members across disciplines
* Generates opportunities (e.g., research, instruction, publication, presentations)
* Promotes team collaboration with colleagues
* Reduces potentially negative turf issues and unproductive competitiveness among faculty members

Students
* Expands students' knowledge of early childhood special education activities within the university (e.g., research projects, grants) and the community
* Enhances access to professionals across disciplines who are active in the field of early childhood special education
* If external funding received, provides opportunities for tuition support
* Provides formal and informal network of contacts who are likely to provide leads for employment opportunities upon graduation
* Affords opportunities for students to observe team collaboration modeled by faculty members across disciplines
* Provides opportunities for students to have a dialogue, negotiate, and learn with students from other disciplines

Administration
* Promotes awareness of and a commitment to the transdisciplinary mission and goals associated with early childhood special education instruction
* Builds on the strengths of faculty members from a variety of disciplines
* Establishes linkages and collaborative activities across departments
* Maximizes the use of resources across departments and programs
* Provides high-quality instruction programs and recommended practices
* Provides cost-effective strategies for addressing personnel needs

Adapted from: Kilgo, J., & Bruder, M. B. (1997). Creating new visions in institutions of higher education: Interdisciplinary approaches to personnel preparation in early intervention. In P. J. Winton, J. A. McCollum, & C. Catlett (Eds.), *Reforming personnel preparation in early intervention: Issues, models, and practical strategies* (pp. 81-101). Baltimore: Paul H. Brookes. Adapted with permission.

Table 12.1

present "real world" situations and challenges faced by professionals as they attempt to deliver transdisciplinary services in the natural environment. Some of the issues and challenges include: How do professionals from various disciplines implement developmentally appropriate practice (DAP) when not all disciplines on the team are familiar with DAP? How can integrated therapy be provided when the general education teachers do not want therapists interfering with their classrooms? What should be done when team members advocate for practices that are in conflict with the family's cultural values? Team-based processes and strategies are utilized to address such issues and challenges.

The various components of *Project TransTeam* at UAB can be seen in Figure 12.1. In addition to the collaborative efforts of faculty and students representing various departments and schools at UAB, *Project TransTeam* involves extensive collaborative efforts with family members and professionals from local agencies (e.g., practicum sites) in rural and urban settings, state agencies (e.g., lead agencies for Part C and Part B-619), and other colleges, universities, and agencies involved in personnel preparation throughout the state and region. Particular emphasis is placed on disseminating information and outcomes of the program to local, state, and national constituents.

Most everyone involved in EI/ECSE realizes that the success or failure of any program for young children with special needs and their families often is dependent upon the quality

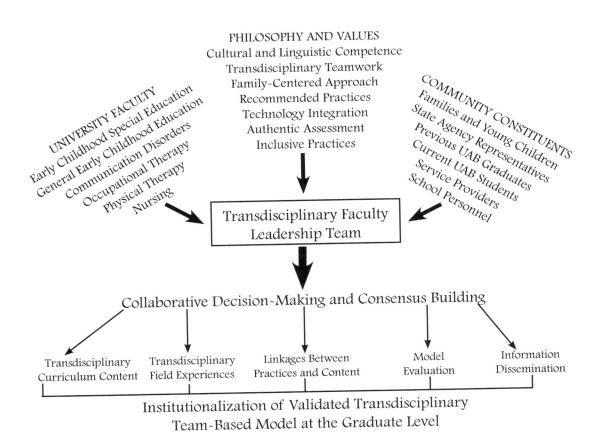

Figure 12.1

of the team of personnel providing services. Therefore, as personnel preparation programs across the United States continue to realign their programs to meet the needs of diverse inclusive educational settings, it becomes increasingly important to move towards transdisciplinary personnel preparation programs in order to prepare high-quality personnel (Kilgo & Bruder, 1997; Stayton et al., 2002). Just as inclusive early childhood environments are the settings of choice to educate young children with disabilities, team-based personnel preparation is the model of choice to produce well-qualified professionals to meet the challenges of the 21st century.

References

Bailey, D. (1996). An overview of interdisciplinary training. In D. Bricker & A. Widerstrom (Eds.), *Preparing personnel to work with infants and young children and their families* (pp. 3-22). Baltimore: Paul H. Brookes.

Kilgo, J., & Bruder, M. B. (1997). Creating new visions in institutions of higher education: Interdisciplinary approaches to personnel preparation in early intervention. In P. J. Winton, J. A. McCollum, & C. Catlett (Eds.), *Reforming personnel preparation in early intervention: Issues, models, and practical strategies* (pp. 81-101). Baltimore: Paul H. Brookes.

Miller, P., & Stayton, V. (2005). Recommended practices in personnel preparation. In S. Sandall, M. L. Hemmeter, B. Smith, & M. McLean (Eds.), *DEC recommended practices: A comprehensive guide for practical application in early intervention/early childhood special education* (pp. 189-220). Longmont, CO: Sopris West.

Stayton, V., Miller, P., & Dinnebeil, L. (2002). *Personnel preparation in early childhood special education.* Longmont, CO: Sopris West.